The Conductor's Score

ELIZABETH A. H. GREEN

Professor Emeritus (Music)
The University of Michigan

NICOLAI MALKO

Internationally Known Conductor

PRENTICE-HALL, INC.   *Englewood Cliffs, New Jersey* 07632

Library of Congress Cataloging-in-Publication Data

GREEN, ELIZABETH A. H.
    The conductor's score.

    Original title: The conductor and his score.
    Bibliography: p. 178.
    Includes indexes.
    1. Conducting.   I. Malko, Nicolai, 1883–1961.
II. Title.
MT85.G77 1985   781.6'33   84-18159
ISBN 0-13-167370-X

Editorial/production supervision: Lisa A. Domínguez
Manufacturing buyer: Ray Keating

0-13-167370-X   01

PRENTICE-HALL INTERNATIONAL, INC. *London*
PRENTICE-HALL OF AUSTRALIA PTY. LIMITED, *Sydney*
EDITORA PRENTICE-HALL DO BRASIL, LTDA., *Rio de Janeiro*
PRENTICE-HALL CANADA INC., *Toronto*
PRENTICE-HALL HISPANOAMERICANA, S.A., *Mexico*
PRENTICE-HALL OF INDIA PRIVATE LIMITED, *New Delhi*
PRENTICE-HALL OF JAPAN, INC., *Tokyo*
PRENTICE-HALL OF SOUTHEAST ASIA PTE. LTD., *Singapore*
WHITEHALL BOOKS LIMITED, *Wellington, New Zealand*

Contents

Foreword   vii

Preface   ix

1

The Next Step in
the Conducting Career   1
Green

*Improving Score Reading   Eye, Ear, and Score
Training the Two Kinds of Hearing   The Often-
Neglected Aspects of Score Study*

2

Psychological Implications
Inherent in the Score   7
Malko

*Conductor, Score, and Instruments   Moral Aspects
of Conducting*

iii

3

Studying the Score   12

Malko

*Instrumentation   Rationalization of the Score
Phrasing   Dynamics   Expression   Style   Quality
Tradition   Philosophical Observations*

4

Marking the Score   30

Malko

*Introduction to Marking   Two Kinds of Score Marking   Richard Strauss' Editing of the Mozart Symphony
in C Major (Jupiter) K 551, first movement*

5

Imagination, Interpretation,
and Memorization   77

Green

*Interpretative Imagination   Applying Interpretative
Imagination   Memory and Memorizing*

6

Rehearsing the Score   91

Malko

*Timing the Rehearsal   Planning the Rehearsal
Conducting the Rehearsal   Beyond the Gesture: Talking   Conductorial Behavior in Rehearsal   For
Whom Do You Perform?*

7

Comments on and Evaluations of Specific Composers 101
Malko

*Stravinsky   Prokofieff   Miaskovsky   Kabalevsky
Glinka   Scriabin   Tchaikovsky   J. Strauss
Letters   Editor's Summation*

8

The Contemporary Score 107
Green

*Historical Background   Contemporary Mores   The
Conductor and His Contemporary Score   Karkoschka's
Research   Grasping the Score Complexities*

9

On Teaching Conducting 125
Green

Building the Conducting Skills   Some Direct Quotations from Malko's Teaching   Some Answers to Pedagogic Questions (Malko)

Appendixes

Appendix A: Review of Transpositions   133

Appendix B: Review of Harmonics and Stringed Instrument Tone Colors   138

Appendix C: *Score Excerpts and Solutions to Problems*   140

Appendix D: Outline Notes on Repertoire   159

*Appendix E: Malko Biographical Material
and Critical Press Notices*   173

Appendix F: Bibliography   178

Indexes

Topical Index   183

Index of Names Mentioned in the Text   188

*Index to Musical Examples,
Charts, and Tables*   190

Foreword

Nicolaï Malko is one of those men who are fortunate—and unfortunate—enough to be born too soon. A pioneer of the technique of conducting, he will remain with Hermann Scherchen, one of the first who understood that the art of conducting, after an empirical period of development, should be based on rational principles. If we are beginning to realize this fact today, we are indebted to a large extent to Nicolaï Malko.

The Conductor and His Baton, his first book, showed the contribution of a remarkably well-organized mind. In this work Malko was endeavoring to evolve a method based on his experience. In this way he is responsible for the emergence of important principles which not only can be transmitted, but are also as easy to follow as those regarding the playing of an instrument. I am thinking of the exercises he suggests and which I never fail to recommend to my students; these exercises make them conscious of what Malko called the "hygiene" of technique. Everything in this book is ingenious and clear, and, far from being an end in itself, technical training appears as the development of the means necessary to serve the score. This is the right, artistic attitude, and it guarantees that the book will never be out of date.

In the second volume, we find the same search for efficiency, but at an even higher level. It deals not with the means available to the conductor to serve the score, but with the inner life of the score itself. Thus a deep and original experience is revealed, and this is what makes the book such fascinating reading. The lights which Malko throws on the works he studies reveal immense knowledge and an approach which is always a lively one. Less systematic than the earlier volume, this book provides an intimate contact with the thought of a great musician. In it Malko appears as a moral example. Both penetrating and humble, he is not afraid to deal with the simplest aspects of his work, from the first contact with the score to the final re-creation at the concert. Thus we are given a wealth of information and of useful approaches, and the teaching of a conductor totally dedicated to the music which he serves.

I thank Mrs. B. Malko and Miss E. Green who by translating and completing this work, made its contents accessible to us. Their faithfulness to the memory of Nicolaï Malko and their exceptional knowledge of the subject provide us with an important contribution in the field of orchestra conducting.

Igor Markevitch
International Conductor
Santa Cecelia Orchestra of Rome

Preface

This volume was originally intended as the second of a two-part work planned and partially executed by Nicolai Malko, the great Russian conductor and teacher of conducting (see Appendix E). The first volume, *The Conductor and his Baton,* was published in English in 1950 by Hansen Verlag, Copenhagen. The second volume, *The Conductor and his Score,* was to have been the sequel. The world of music suffered an irreparable loss when Malko died before the second book was finished.

Under the guidance and advice of Dr. Malko's widow, Mrs. Berthe Malko, the present author has continued the writing for the second volume, adding necessary material where the Malko notes were incomplete and, in so doing bringing the book into line and format to act concomitantly as a sequel to the widely used textbook, *The Modern Conductor*. This new volume on score study may be used in advanced conducting classes.

The first Malko volume dealt with the mastery of the controlling and expressive gestures of the conductor—the silent language of the stick which is "read" by the musicians of the ensemble, at times almost instinctively rather than consciously. *The Modern Conductor,* published ten years later, and based on the Malko teaching techniques, became a textbook for the student just starting on his serious study of the conductor's art. The two books parallel each other, the Malko book approaching the problems from the standpoint of the professional conductor, *The Modern Conductor* adapting to the college textbook approach. The latter includes, in addition to the manual technique, certain elementary score-study information needed by the novice conductor.

It is not the intent here to duplicate material from either *The Con-*

ductor and His Baton or *The Modern Conductor,* but rather to go on now from where they left off.

Once a young conductor's basic manual technique has become functional, his future lies in the building of repertoire and the refining of his "elementary" experience.

There is no great mass of literary material available dealing with the live performance of the score. Score study alone does not guarantee a great performance. The psychology of the contact between conductor and musicians, the handling of the rehearsal hours, and the final presentation before the live audience all need parallel attention. It is hoped that this volume will fill a gap in this aspect of the conductor's life, especially for the student who continues his study beyond the first year of conducting instruction.

Malko often spoke of the baton technique as the "grammar" and the score study as the "syntax" of the language, the latter elevating the grammar to literary heights, abstracting from the printed symbols the deeper meaning behind them.

Countless times the maestro stressed that the vital reason for perfecting the grammar (the technique of the baton) was to be able to express clearly, concisely, and vitally the emotional content (the meaning) of the printed page. "It is not enough to study a score thoroughly. One should also know how to conduct it, and should prepare his gestures as well." The musicians of the ensemble, the "live" instrument, should be able to understand instantly the conductor's intent and through his gestures be enabled to respond at the peak of their artistic ability. Any struggle to interpret an ambiguous gesture handicaps artistic performance.

"I do not see anything inconsistent with speaking about the necessity for technical preparation for the conductor, the goal being the best rendition in living sound of the creation of the composer."

The black and white symbols in the score are the composer's attempt to record his inspiration. They are what the conductor studies with utmost sincerity and from every angle in order to make his "translation" as authentic and interesting as possible.

"The important thing is not whether the composer is living, but whether his *music* is alive. There are, in fact, living composers whose music is, on the contrary, quite dead."

Malko's notes were written in his native language, Russian. The translations were done by Mrs. Malko, who also provided the biographical material, dates, and press releases from the Malko archives. Her dedicated efforts have made this book possible.

Chapters 1, 5, 8, and 9 are additions to the original Malko notes. Chapter 5, however, is based on memory-outlining principles as suggested by the maestro. Quotations from Malko appear as indicated in the chapters written by Green. Whenever the first person is used (it appears in the Malko chapters), it is Malko himself speaking. The phrasal analysis of the Borodin Second Symphony is taken directly from one of Dr. Malko's study scores, and the outlines for specific repertoire, found in Appendix D, also bear the Malko imprint.

Quoting again from the maestro, "The young conductor, after conquering time beating and the many interpretative gestures and controls necessary for leading the musicians, must next learn how to proceed from time beating to interpretation. He must learn how to solve the problems of the score, how to rehearse the difficult spots, how to see in the score itself why they are difficult, and finally to know what to do about them. . . .

"One is permitted to interpret (the score), to make clear the content, but not to rewrite. The inspiration behind the score belongs to the composer. The conductor—the performer—recreates.

"Style concerns itself with the exactness with which a composer's intentions are conveyed in the subsequent performance. The *truth* is in the *score*."

Appreciation is expressed to Carl J. Alexius and Gary D. Cook for helpful suggestions.

For the reader who is not familiar with the Malko name, Appendix E will provide the necessary statistics and give some idea of the impact this man has had on twentieth-century conducting and the teaching of the art. Malko became a United States citizen in 1946.

Elizabeth A. H. Green

"The *truth* is in the *score*."

Nicolai Malko

chapter 1

The Next Step in

the Conducting Career

Green

It is now taken for granted that the reader of this book will have completed his introduction to the manual art of the conductor: his baton technique should have become functional as well as his understanding of the basics of instrumentation, transposition, and score format.

In preparing for a career, the young conductor turns next to the intensive study of scores and the building of a large and permanent repertoire. His future success will depend on how well the musicians are handled, on the skillful and audience-inspiring renditions of the music, and on the size and interest of the repertoire performed.

The score and its production into living sound henceforth become the center of attention.

IMPROVING SCORE READING

It may seem elementary to remind ourselves that each symbol in music stands *simultaneously* for two concepts—the pitch to be sounded and how long each sound should last. Very subtly this tells us that progress in score skills should go in two directions, namely, the eye-mind skill of quicker score analysis and the ear-mind improvement of the silent hearing of the notated music.

In entering the advanced conducting class, the young conductor has already become accustomed to the perpendicular lining up of beats as a basic factor in score reading. He sees instantly the rhythmic relationships of the several parts. He understands his score in block form by families

1

of instruments, and melodic interest undoubtedly is quickly located. Cross accents have emerged into the consciousness. Stress has been laid on variation of rhythm and balance between the melody line and the accompanying figures. His glance also encompasses instantly the important dynamic markings. Familiarity with transpositions has enabled him to recognize the various instruments on the page simply by their key signatures. (If review is needed, Appendix A may help.)

Building on such a foundation, the next stage of development will be concerned with three broad problems: technically, increasing the *spontaneous* proficiency of eye, ear, and manual technique; musically, challenging to the utmost the imagination in its interpretative powers; and psychologically, the problem of how best to deal with the musicians themselves.

Painting, sculpture, and architecture are *art in space*. Music is *art in time*—something *heard* at the moment and then disappearing into the ether once its moment of sounding has passed.

The greater the conductor, the greater his ability to hear. When he studies scores, he applies himself to hearing in his mind the melodic line, the harmony, and the sound or color of each instrument as it adds its voice to the ensemble. Constantly imagining the sound, he builds an ideal in his mind. When he rehearses the orchestra, he tries to produce audibly the realization of his imagined ideal. *Objective hearing* and *imaginative* (or *subjective*) *hearing* complement each other. (These are Malko's terms.) Both kinds of hearing are necessary, and woe be to the conductor who is weak in either! Toscanini's imagined ideal was so sublime that he often became frustrated in rehearsal when he could not immediately get the orchestra to render audibly this idealized sound.

EYE, EAR, AND SCORE

While the eye and ear constantly aid each other in the score-reading process, one might say that the eye tends toward correlating the rhythmic problems and the ear, the problems of pitch, color, and balance. Vertical reading of the score encompasses the rhythmic synchronization and the harmony, but melody line and phrasing are read by the horizontal extension of the beats.

In the phrase, the beats lead toward a temporary climax or a temporary termination. Phrasal consciousness on the part of the conductor is one of the vital factors in clarifying the rendition for the audience. Malko deals with this in Chapter 4, page 35.

TRAINING THE TWO KINDS OF HEARING

For the ear, things are complicated. The two kinds of hearing have been mentioned: *the objective hearing of audible sounds* and the *subjective, imagined, inner-ear process.*

Objective hearing is easily trained. One has only to concentrate his attention on what is actually sounding. The attitude should be one of positive criticism, taking pleasure and delight in the fine performance and applying one's own intelligence and musicianship to *solving the problems* of the less than adequate renditions. A negative criticism of what is sounding should always be accompanied by a positive idea of how to remedy the fault.

Training the *imaginative hearing* is much more complex and difficult. It needs a great deal of specialized attention. If the reader should feel a weakness in this facet of his work, perhaps the following anecdote will help him to locate consciously this inner-ear hearing.

Not long ago a college professor sat at the piano testing the sight-singing ability of a young man in the conducting class, a college junior. Although the student's performance on his major instrument was outstanding, he made far too many mistakes in singing the written line of music, especially when there were interval skips.

An experiment was tried: An E-natural was played on the piano. The student was told, "Do not sing this pitch. Now, without singing the E, THINK the sound of F-sharp, one whole tone higher. WAIT! Do you *feel* the pitch forming in the back of your head?" After a moment he said in astonishment, "Yes!"

"So now sing the F-sharp." He did so, perfectly. (The vocal cords can perform ONLY what the mind has thought correctly first.)

Looking at the professor in amazement, the young man exclaimed, "Do you know that's the first time in my life that has ever happened to me!"

"Well, son, now you have found your inner ear—an absolute necessity for the conductor."

Imagined-pitch identification is an elementary step in ear training. In order of sequence, the process is as follows: (1) to be able to imagine accurately a whole tone or half tone, either up or down, from any pitch sounded; (2) then to be able to sing all notes of the *scale* that are *missing between intervals* without switching to a different key in the process; (3) finally, to be able to carry those missing notes in the inner ear, singing audibly only the terminal notes of the interval. When these three processes are performed without error, the inner ear is ready for score use.

The problem is obviously one for the mind, the imaginative hearing, rather than the singing voice. It is a truism that until a student can first hear accurately "in the back of his head," there is not much hope of his developing a fine imaginative hearing for his score study problems.

At a conductor's symposium in the Netherlands, the members of the professional orchestra inserted wrong notes here and there, as a drill for the conductors present. At first the mistakes were glaring ones, but they became more subtle as the young conductors improved. This is an excellent way to correlate objective hearing with imaginative hearing.

A young conductor on the way up will sometimes be given the opportunity of conducting a community or non-professional orchestra as part of his training. In such an organization, intonation is often a problem. It is good to remember that the ear hears most quickly the highest pitch sounded. In tuning the orchestra, one should be aware of this fact. The highest pitch may not be the correct one. Therefore, one must concentrate on the standard and not be misled by a subtle sharping of the sound.

THE OFTEN NEGLECTED ASPECT OF SCORE STUDY

Once the music of the score has been fully assimilated, the conductor would do well to think through how he is going to show it to the performers. His gestures can often either make or break him. In Appendix C, the reader will find one score fully edited with gestures. A needed gesture is chosen to make life easier for the players, not because of a whim of the conductor.

Supplementary Readings *(See Appendix F)*

G. W. Cooper and L. B. Meyer, *The Rhythmic Structure of Music.*
Gordon Jacob, *How to Read a Score,* Chapter VI, "Aural Imagination."
Emil Kahn, *Conducting,* Part II, "The Ear and the Eye."
Robert A. Melcher and Willard F. Warch, *Music for Score Reading.*
Warwick Braithwait, *The Conductor's Art.*

Exercises for Practice *(Training the Imaginative Hearing)*

1. Strike any note on the piano. Without singing it, THINK the sound of a whole tone above (or below) it. When the pitch forms in the imagination, sing it and check it against the piano. Do a series of notes in this way until it becomes easy.

2. Do the same with the half step.

3. Repeat the above exercises on many different pitches. Try to practice daily. Imaginative hearing grows as it is used.

4. Sing a scale. Then take an interval from the scale, such as the third note to the sixth note, and scalewise sing the notes that are missing between the first and last notes of the interval. Try the second note of the scale to the seventh note, singing the missing notes. Be sure to remain in the original key throughout. Do not sing notes that are not present in the given scale.

5. Take one part—preferably *not* the melody line—of any three- or four-part song. Sing slowly, not worrying about rhythmic accuracy, filling in all missing notes in each interval skip. Check with the piano after each note is sung in order to be sure that you are singing within the given key.

   Caution: Students often make the mistake of slipping over into the key of the *first note of the interval,* as if that note were the key note of a scale. Thus

Example A

Sing down the scale from D to F-sharp. Be sure that you sing the G-sharp belonging to the key of A major and not the G-natural of the key of D major. Remain in the key of A major throughout.

Example B

In Example B, sing in the key of D minor from D up to A; add the whole tone, B-natural; then sing down from A to the E while remaining in the key of D minor. Do not sing G-sharp and F-sharp as if a modulation had occurred when the B-natural entered.

6. Once you have mastered the scale approach, then try hearing the

intermediary notes (between the terminal notes of the interval) in the imagination, singing audibly only the terminal notes of the interval. Check results on the piano for accuracy.

7. Take a score. *Sing only the first note in any given measure.* Sing upward from the lowest to the highest score-line, placing each note within your vocal range. Use the scale routine when the interval from one part to the next bothers you. Make the necessary transpositions as called for in the score.

8. Since the harmony usually changes on the first beat of the measure in Haydn and Mozart scores, choose a score and apply the method of Exercise 7 above. Sing the first note of each measure, progressing vertically upward through the score until the top line is reached. Then take the first note of the next measure and do the same. It makes an excellent exercise.

Imaginative hearing improves through practice. We learn to imagine pitch by daily practice on exercises such as those given above.

chapter 2

Psychological Implications

Inherent in the Score

Malko

Conducting as an art has been steadily developing during the last hundred years. The original pedagogic and administrative aspects have continued, but other facets of conducting, such as the educational and creative, are increasing rapidly. The conductor of today cannot be only a musician. He must be an active person, vital, alive, and he must, above all, be an artist-performer, musically and technically.

He is in control during the performance, listening intently to the intonation and adjusting the balance of the instruments for the auditorium in which the performance is taking place. It might be said that the situation would be ideal if this superimposed control were not necessary, but that rarely happens. Necessary as the control is, a conductor, however, makes a serious mistake if he permits the "controller" to overshadow the "artist" within himself.

CONDUCTOR, SCORE, AND INSTRUMENTS

The conductor acts as a guide, a solver of problems, a decision maker. His guidance chart is the composer's score; his job, to animate the score, to make it come alive, to bring it into audible being.

To do this he familiarizes himself with every nook and cranny of the topography as set forth in his guidance chart. His imagination is ever active as he plans his route, foreseeing possible trouble spots along the way and deciding beforehand how to solve the problems that may arise.

As a conductor studies his scores he soon realizes that he will deal with three kinds of instruments: the human voice (the "natural" instrument); the "dead" instrument (constructed by men and made of wood, metal, ivory, or skins); and the multi-headed "living" instrument (the chorus, orchestra, or band).

Independent of the quality of each, their peculiarities are as follows:

The Voice

One may call the voice the natural instrument. The voice is distinctive in that it has an immediate connection with the will. The singer is not conscious of changing the shape of his vocal cords as he performs. In fact, he could not do so even if he tried. He simply wills the sound and the sound comes forth. In one way this is an advantage because such a process is the result of and dependent on life itself. But in art one must do more than just exist, more than just be alive. One must add to his existence some kind of conscious effort—and this creates a paradox. The voice, being innate and fundamentally unchangeable, becomes thereby a less grateful instrument in the sense of the ultimate control of the performance. There are, for example, voices that do not lend themselves to truly artistic performance because of their innate qualities. The genuinely great voice is an accident of nature.

The Dead Instrument

The dead instrument is constructed by man and is made of wood, metal, ivory, or skins. The mastery of such an instrument is the mastery of its technique. Everything is, philosophically, easier. Thus it has been possible for man to perfect the instrument itself. It has also been possible to perfect the theory of performance thereon. Schools of pedagogy have developed; pedagogic methods and directions have matured. Styles of technique have come into existence. All of these are teachable.

The Living Instrument

The chorus, orchestra, or band, comprised of living human beings, is the most complicated *mixtum compositum*. The chorus has the advantage of the immediate response, a living instrument within a living person. In artistic performance the voice must be trained away from its natural impulse, namely, its impulse to depict how the human being is feeling at the moment; instead, it must present the spirit of the music being performed.

In the orchestra we have an alive instrument without this immediate connection with the center of will. Instead, here is a conglomerate of dead instruments in the hands of living persons who themselves, in turn, become living instruments.

In speaking of the piano, violin, or other instrument, we often use expressions such as "a sensitive instrument," "like a living instrument," or "as if the instrument had come alive." If this intimate contact between the performer and the dead instrument is a necessary premise of the artistic performance, it becomes clear that this factor acquires a special significance when in front of the musician-performer (the conductor in this case) is found a multi-headed, living instrument (the members of the orchestra). The contact between musician-performer and instrument now takes on vast psychological implications. The conductor must depend on his own ability to create a contact, a rapport, between himself and the members of the chorus, orchestra, or band. This contact should be of a quality to guarantee an intense concentration on the part of the artists of the ensemble and endow them with the desire to understand and assimilate the conductor's intentions, embodying them into the sound, and thus preserving the integrity of the score, the culture and performing gift of the conductor, and the corresponding musicianship of each member of the performing group. This aspect holds an important place in the work of every conductor—a significance no less important than the relationship between a teacher and his pupils or between a commander and his soldiers.

Moreover, if an instrument made of wood or metal has its own limits of endurance (the strings of a piano breaking with some overly enthusiastic pianists; the scratching sound emitted by the string of a violin when the bow has been pressed too heavily; the disruption of sound when forced on a wind instrument; the bursting skin under the sticks of a too violent timpanist), it should be a warning to the conductor. When the dead instruments thus object, how much more sensitive are the living instruments, the human members of the ensemble! In addition to everything else, they have to convey the artistic wishes of the conductor and reconcile them with their own artistic concepts, tempered, complemented, and corrected by means of the dead instruments functioning in their hands.

The psychological implications of this arrangement are infinite. We shall confine ourselves now to only those that are of practical importance for the conductor as they relate to deciding his fate (and the composer's!) in his rehearsals, concerts, and theatrical performances.

MORAL ASPECTS OF CONDUCTING

Conducting has both its mental side and moral side. The mental side deals with the intensive study of the score; the moral side concerns the relationship between conductor and musicians. We are interested here in the moral side from the purely practical or professional standpoint. I would consider thoughtless and pharisaic the objections that might be brought forth concerning our dealing with this question. *To realize the printed score in its full majesty requires a certain musical and artistic rapport between the conductor and his musicians.*

On one hand, there are conductors who may be basically wonderful people and who have thoroughly mastered their score, but they cannot establish the necessary contact with their players; they do not know how to work with an orchestra or chorus, and their results are therefore inferior to their innate abilities as artist-performers. There are, on the other hand, conductors who are not nice human beings but who do know how to get along with an ensemble and how to obtain its cooperation, and they do it without special effort or immoral means.

The attention of the student can be directed to specific cases. For example, he may be advised to imitate one conductor in a positive way and to learn from another conductor what not to do. Here I would like to make a few deductions and indulge in some generalizations on how to work with live people. Certain conclusions may be drawn as to what is the best way, at least from the professional point of view. Eventually, this becomes a question of moral conduct because it is, I think, fundamentally impossible to deceive a human being.

The best performance of an orchestra or chorus is that which reveals its own possibilities as well as the maximum possibilities of the score. The performance is the result of the preliminary work done in the rehearsals plus the phenomenon of "coming alive" that takes place in the performance. Here we stumble over all sorts of complications and negations. To begin with, the conductor and orchestra have to be genuinely conductor and orchestra. They both have to possess the necessary technical and artistic qualities. Since there are no purely ideal phenomena in life, the very best conductor with the very best orchestra will at times outshine the sun, but at other times they may cause spots to appear. But it is not uncommon to find, at times, a good orchestra in the hands of a mediocre conductor, and vice versa. The corresponding weaknesses handicap the work. As a result, rehearsals may not take place under ideal conditions and the ultimate realization of the composer's directives may leave much to be desired.

It is the conductor's job to obtain the maximum under any circumstances regardless of what attendant circumstances may interfere: lack of rehearsal time, poor conditions of the printed parts, sickness of an orchestra member and the consequent undesirable replacement. The audience is not concerned with these matters. It does, however, have the right to expect and to demand the best of performances.

The responsibility for everything rests on the shoulders of the conductor. His role begins here, where, in addition to his purely musical ability and talent, his characteristics as pedagogue and administrator, together with his whole personality, play a tremendous part.

There is a terrible misconception acquired by many "bosses" in all domains including the arts that "this is what I am and everybody will have to cope with it." This attitude is wrong, stupid, and even criminal.

It is impossible to change one's fundamental nature, but one can and should learn to rid himself of many shortcomings by imposing a proper and professional self-control.

As long as disposition takes part in the professional work, it should respond to professional standards. This does not mean that one should pretend to be what he is not, should be untruthful, or should smile insincerely. It does mean that one should observe the elementary rules of human decency both in the contacts of daily life and under working conditions.

To bring the music to full fruition—to breathe life into the symbols on the printed page—a conductor and his musicians work cooperatively together toward one ultimate goal: the finest possible musical realization of the score.

Supplementary Readings *(See Appendix F)*

CHARLES BLACKMAN, *Behind the Baton:* Chapter 8, "Psychology"; Chapter 10, "What the Musicians Expect from the Conductor."
PETER PAUL FUCHS, *The Psychology of Conducting.*

Problems: *What would you do if*

1. A wrong note is heard?
2. A player tells you, "I can't read your beat"?
3. The melody line is not clearly heard?
4. Indifference, restlessness, and inattention are manifest when you stop rehearsing in order to speak to the musicians?
5. Wrong entrances are made?

See page 156 for suggested solutions.

chapter 3

Studying the Score

Malko

The thought occurs that the peculiar *par excellence* emotionality of music is the reason for the neglect of the thorough study and theorizing that the score should have before it is conducted.

The instrumentalist is prone to do his studying by grabbing his instrument and beginning to play the notes. Often he would be farther ahead if he would first take some time to read through the part without the instrument, giving his mind a chance to grasp what is to come.

For the conductor, the mental side of his work is an absolute prerequisite. Presenting himself before an orchestra or chorus before he has thoroughly studied his score and done the necessary theoretical preparation is like an actor coming onto the stage without having read his lines beforehand. He would repeat the words of the prompter automatically, understanding only later their sense and meaning.

The conductor must first read the music mentally, think it over, study it, and then finally come to the audible sound. Too often he first hears the sound—in a performance somewhere or via a recording—and is so influenced by what he has heard that he becomes an imitator rather than a creative artist. If the performance he has heard is good, this should be remembered, but if the performance is bad, surely he should not imitate it. However, even in the case of a good performance, the habit of imitating paralyzes one's own individuality.

If the young musician listens many times to only one performance, he unconsciously accepts the bad with the good. He accepts the mistakes and the "traditions" without question, takes over the job of performing the music, and his musicians very quickly realize that the rehearsal is for his own benefit rather than theirs. The result: the live instrument sleeps through the rehearsal. The conductor's preparation should be much more elaborate as the reader will see in this and the following chapters.

So let us now proceed to the question: how does one study score?

INSTRUMENTATION

First, the conductor looks at the instrumentation (the first page of the score or the movement). How many instruments and which ones are needed for the performance of the work?

Obviously, the conductor must learn the music itself, the notes on the page. For this purpose he often resorts to the piano, transposing the several parts so that the sound will be correct, placing them in his mind into the right octave, hearing the orchestral color of each instrument with his inner ear as he translates it to the piano. Recordings may also help, but here imitation is in danger of taking over.

But knowing the notes and the instrumentation is not enough. The conductor must understand the *content* of the music. This includes the style, the emotional character, the structural peculiarities (of form, phrasing, harmony, and of the technique of the individual instruments) plus the recognition of the problems that must be dealt with in the rehearsal. These problems may be technical in relation to the instruments; they may be concerned with difficult rhythms, with passages that may be out of balance when performed by the prospective orchestra; they may be concerned with the actual baton work, namely, how best to show the music through gesture. The conductor should consciously think through what the written notes and directions tell him so that his gestures make these directions and their meaning clear for the players.

One can say that when a conductor studies the score he is studying "in translation." Just as it is possible to translate French well without having written the work, so it is possible to translate the symbols in a musical score into sound without having been the author of these symbols. In learning to speak a foreign language the accent, dialect, and local expressions are often mistaken for the pure language itself. In music it is the same. The sounds that have been heard (in a performance, on a recording, or even in a rehearsal) tend to represent the music. They may not have been the actual sounds written or requested by the composer. The student of the score has accepted a certain meaning for the symbols, but it may not necessarily be the right or best meaning. One must always retain respect for the composer's rights.

RATIONALIZATION OF THE SCORE

The rationalization of the score—the mental approach to it before it turns into live sound—might be termed the practice on a silent keyboard.

Certainly, the most violent enemy of "too great rationalization," with its attendant dryness and technicalities, would not deny the advantage that a cultured and scientific basis for study and performance has in contrast to a dilettantish approach. This presupposes, as always, that the two conductors in question have an equal amount of musical talent.

A work of visual art has its center of interest, it moments of quiet, its peaks of passion, its contours from small hills to highest mountains. Musically, all such things are delineated in the conductor's score with the same forethought as that of the painter who gradually puts his picture on canvas.

It is well to study the score first with the broad view. It is the panoramic view, the taking in of the whole scene, paying attention to the forest instead of the individual trees. Read through the score as though it were a literary work.

PHRASING

Just as the forest is comprised of many single trees, so the music is divided into phrases—the grouping of bars. Clarifying the measure grouping, counting it out by phrases from first measure to last, often reveals hidden surprises to the conductor. Certainly, it clarifies his understanding and ability to memorize, especially in the difficult places where the conducting is dangerous.

Analysis of every musical fragment of the score can be presented in a graphic scheme in which each motif, each phrase, bar, or group of bars show their relationship to one another. Such an analysis is very useful, especially in complicated music (See Chart I).

Chart I: Phrasal Analysis by Measures, Bartok, Concerto for Orchestra, first movement (Malko)

Phrasal Analysis by Measures　　　　　　　Bartok: Concerto for Orchestra,
　　　　(Malko)　　　　　　　　　　　　　　　　first movement

5 - 4 - 2 $\boxed{12}$ - 4 - 4 - 2 $\boxed{22}$ - 7 - 6 - $\boxed{35}$ - 4 - 5 - 3 - 4 $\boxed{51}$ - 4 - 3 - 3^{timp} - 2 -

4 - 3 - 3^{fl} - 3 $\boxed{76}$ - 6 - 4 - 4 - 1^{rit} - 3 - 1 - 4 - 3 - $\boxed{102}$ - 7 - 3$\boxed{110}$ - 3 - 3 -

3 - 3 $\boxed{122}$ w.w. - 1 - 4 - 2 - 5　tbni - 7 - 8 $\boxed{149}$ - 5 - 1 $\boxed{155}$ - 4 - 1 - 4 - 1 -
　　　　　　　strg　3 - 3 - 3 - 3 -　(1 - 6)

$\boxed{165}$ - 6 - 3^{harp} - 1 $\boxed{175}$ - 2 - 1 - 2 - 1 $\boxed{181}$ - 6 - 5 $\boxed{192}$ - 2 - 1 - 2 - 1 - $\boxed{198}$ - 6 -
　　(9)

4 - 2 $\boxed{210}$ - 2 - 4 - 3 - 2 - 3 - 7^{celli} - $\boxed{231}$ - 1 - 1 - 4 - 1 - 1 - 3 $\boxed{242}$ - 6 - 6 -
　　　　　　　　　　　(6)

4 - 7 - 7 $\boxed{272}$ - 6 - 6 - 4 $\boxed{288}$ - 6 - 6 - 3 - 3 - 3 - 4 $\boxed{313}$ - 3 - 6 - 6 - 6 - 6 - 2

$\boxed{342}$ - 6 - 5 - 5 - 5 - 3 -$^{\text{tbni (2)}}$ 2 -^{tbni} 8 - 4 $\boxed{380}$ - 6 $\boxed{386}$ - 4 - 6 $\boxed{396}$ - 5 - 1 - 5

1 - 5 $\boxed{413}$ - 1 - 5 - 5 $\boxed{424}$ - 1 - 4 - 4 - 5 - 6^{harp} - 3 - 2 - 2^{fl} 2 - 3 $\boxed{456}$ - 6 - 5^{trpt}

$\boxed{467}$ - 3 - 2 - 2 - 2 $\boxed{476}$ - 4 - 8　Temp. I　- 6 - 2 - 1 - 2 - 2 - 1 - 2 - 1 - 2 - 2

$\boxed{509}$ - 5 - 6 - 2

Reference Music for Chart I: Bartok, Concerto for Orchestra, first movement, measures 1–30 and 122–142.

I
(INTRODUZIONE)

Notice the double line of analysis in the Chart concerning measures 122–142.

When this type of phrasal analysis is conscientiously studied out for each composition to be performed, the conductor will find that he notices many subtleties that would otherwise not call themselves to his attention.

It is not intended that these phrasal numbers be memorized as such. This process of analysis is for study purposes, for clarifying the music in the conductor's mind, and for giving him one very necessary means, among many, of approaching his score. His readings subtly become more intelligible to his audiences—a gratifying and worthy result for the time spent in this serious endeavor.

The reader will find a detailed analysis of this process in Chapter 4, Marking the Score, page 35.

In perusing the next two musical examples, the reader will understand the value of this process and its immediate influence on his efficiency.

Let us look now at Borodin's Second Symphony, first movement (Musical Example 3–1).

Musical Example 3–1: Borodin, Second Symphony, first movement, measures 1–11 compared with measures 25–37. (Melody line only quoted.)

(a) Measures 1–11

(b) Measures 25–37

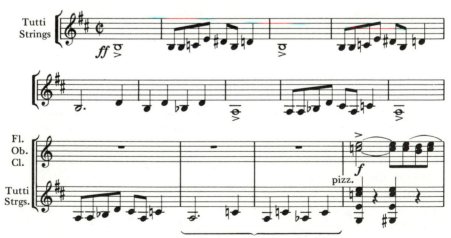

Two extra measures here

Measures 35 and 36 of the example are *added* before the strings take
the chords and the woodwinds enter with the melodic line. Careful analysis, phrasally and measurewise, helps to prevent the conductor from
giving a wrong cue to the woodwinds on their second melodic entrance.
The stated measures could easily have been overlooked if the conductor
had not "counted out" his phrases.

Consider also Mozart's *Overture to The Impresario* with its measure
groupings in threes (Musical Example 3–2).

Musical Example 3–2: Mozart, Overture to *The Impresario,* measures 1–6.

Note: Whole passage then repeats

This careful phrasal analysis is too often neglected in score study.

In writing the score the composer has used symbols to set forth his
ideas. Within the limits of his ability he has left a written record of his
inspiration. The score is the only clue the conductor has on how the
music should sound and it is up to him to ferret it out by every means
at his disposal. Phrasal analysis is one of the vital means. In studying
the score the conductor is communing with the mind of the composer
and, after all, the composer is the one who has created the music and
has indicated what is to be done with it.

Some composers take fancies to particular instruments and show a
preference for them in their compositions. Some stress the brasses and

write especially well for them. Others may show an interest in the harp or the percussion or the viola tone. These composers become known for their preferences. Similarly, some conductors get carried away by, for example, dynamics, or tempo (always too fast), or cueing. They become known as "dynamics conductors" or "tempo conductors" or "cueing conductors." Over-emphasis in any one direction is not good. The comprehensive truth lies in the score itself and the final goal is the music.

DYNAMICS

Every phrase, even the shortest one, has its expression—either an onrush (a forward direction) or a backlash (a terminal feeling). Music is in constant motion, usually creating a demand for prolonged action, a feeling that the phrase in itself is a continuation of the motion.

Interpretatively, phrasal handling is most often connected with variation in dynamics. This does not, however, negate a pertinent, very gentle, modification of the tempo when the musical feeling demands it. Both tempo and dynamics contribute to clarifying the phrasing.

A conductor must *lead* a phrase and build a structure out of phrases. He should discern the initial elements and distinguish them from the subsequent ones, not smoothing everything down to a dead level or to an identical form of expression.

Although tempo and dynamics individualize and differentiate phrases, still more important is the ever-changing character of the music itself. Music is never static. It flows through time. Life is never static either. Each moves constantly forward toward its conclusion. When either becomes motionless, monotony sets in and finally existence ceases.

EXPRESSION

Score study also means giving concentrated attention to the expression. The technical means for expression are tempo, dynamics, legato and non-legato. Individually and in combination they give the conductor an almost infinite variety with whch to show the change of character from phrase to phrase. A dead-level, monotonous performance is a tragedy. It is as if the conductor has presented us with a paper on the formal analysis of the work instead of an inspired artistic representation.

In making the transition from tempo to tempo, from phrase to phrase, dynamic to dynamic, the line of the music must not be broken. This has to do with the conductor's own musicality and his control of his conductorial technique. Suffice it to say that to realize fully the expressive aspects of the score, the baton must have as full a range of expression as any individual instrumentalist has on his dead instrument. The dynamic and kinetic exaggerations, the upward crescendo, the downward diminuendo, the fermata-tenuto, and the non-legatos (staccatos that are like the pricks of a pin)—all of these should be skillfully shown by the easy and facile baton of the conductor. (What orchestra would hire a player who was incapable of playing a clean staccato when the music demanded it, but yet, with the baton . . . ?)

STYLE

Style concerns itself with the exactness with which a composer's intentions are conveyed in the subsequent performance. Here again the truth is in the score.

Once I remarked to Stravinsky, "In my opinion you descend not from Mozart, not from Beethoven, but from Haydn," to which he replied, "Of course I descend from Haydn."

Style encompasses both the personal approach of the composer to his composition and the general period and kind of music prevalent during his lifetime. The conductor must acquire a feeling and understanding for both.

Take, for example, the music of Sibelius. His music is popular in the United States. (Some say it is because Finland was the only country that paid its debts to the United States after the war! But there is a more pertinent reason.) Sibelius belongs to those few composers who know how to compose symphonies. He has a gift for creating his musical thoughts in big forms. He does not violate his thought for the sake of the form and does not violate the form for the sake of the thought. His creation is natural and organic. This does not mean that his music is perfect, but it does mean that the listener not only hears his music but also listens to it.

It is not unusual to hear remarks of a philosophic character used as excuses either to conceal defects in a performance or to justify a denial of the composer's intentions. For example, a person is strong and healthy, full-blooded—and he makes everything sound that way. He approaches the score from the sound. He cannot stand "all of the talk about style." Another person is an exaggerated individualist. He prides himself on performing "what is not written in the score." This is a very dangerous region since it often accounts for unmusical distortions. The excuse given for this philosophy is Liszt's statement that "the important may not be written into the score." However, Liszt's remark was never meant to imply the unlimited right of every performer to distort to the point of rebuilding.

QUALITY

The idea of creative performance is immensely elastic. Meyerhold, the stage director, used to say, "When a performance is more talented it convinces." What was he trying to prove? The quality of the work itself or the quality of the performance? One should be extremely careful not to confuse these two ideas. In principle they are both independent and heterogeneous. It is just as impossible to substitute one for the other as it is to substitute a pound for a yard or a kilo for a meter.

We must consider quality in the light of the compounding of its fractions. We can elicit facts like these: This composition has defects in form but they are compensated for by the beauty of the themes, their development, their orchestration, and so on. Each facet may counterbalance the others. In art there are no trifles. Everything is of paramount importance.

TRADITION

When a tradition that is obviously bad has become established, the conductor should diligently fight against it, both in large and in small things. For example, in the Fifth Symphony of Dvorak two things are traditionally misplayed: There is no sforzato in measure 89 of the third movement, and in measures 62 and 63 there are no forte-pianos, yet one hears them constantly in performance (Musical Examples 3–3 and 3–4).

Musical Example 3–3: Dvorak, Fifth Symphony, third movement, measures 84–86 and 88–90.

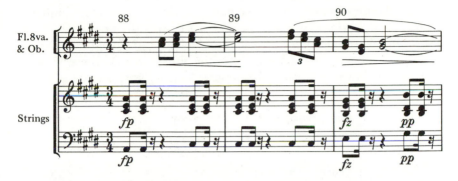

Musical Example 3–4: Dvorak, Fifth Symphony, third movement, measures 60–63.

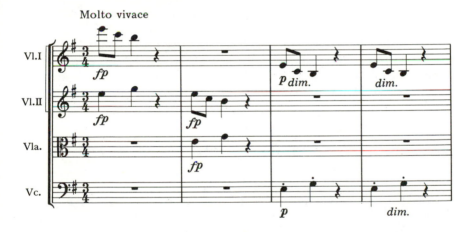

In classical music the transition from one tempo to another was not emphasized as such. It is better to get into the tempo *before* the main theme starts. Thus in Mozart's Jupiter Symphony, K 551, in the fourth movement, the tempo of the recapitulation should be set in the measures just preceding it, measures 223 and 224 (Musical Example 3–5).

Musical Example 3–5: Mozart, Symphony in C Major (Jupiter), K 551, fourth movement, measures 223–228.

The application of style to the music and its accompanying influence on quality of performance may be concerned with the manner in which a surrounding counterpoint is related to the known melody line. Nikisch [1] performed the staccato sixteenths on the flutes and clarinets *senza espressione* as shown in Musical Example 3–6.

Musical Example 3–6: Tchaikovsky, Fourth Symphony, second movement, measures 85–86.

It is in bad taste to make a crescendo after a chord fermata. When such an effect is necessary, it will be so indicated by the composer, as Stravinsky did at the end of the *Firebird Suite*. Following the ffff, the last three bars should be performed *pp subito,* crescendo, sfff as marked (Musical Example 3–7).

Musical Example 3–7: Stravinsky, *Firebird Suite,* last 8 measures.

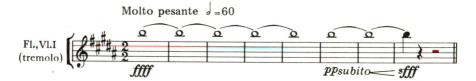

Copyright, 1920, J. & W. Chester, Ltd., London. Used by permission of the copyright owners, J. & W. Chester, Ltd.

PHILOSOPHICAL OBSERVATIONS

It is possible for a brilliant performance to cover the inadequacies of the music itself. It is also possible for the message of a great composition to shine through a mediocre performance. One sometimes wonders why it is that he hears fine performances of poor music but more often

[1] Arthur Nikisch (1855–1922), the Toscanini of his time. Malko had played certain performances under his baton.

he hears mediocre performances of great music. True, it is more difficult to deal with good music than it is with bad. For those who really love "serious music" it sometimes speaks for itself; the performance cannot ruin it completely. But this should not satisfy the performer. One should aim always for the best possible performance, qualitywise, and not rely entirely on the genius of the composer.

Doboujinsky [2] used to say, "The most important thing in Art is to shorten, to abridge . . . but for this one must create much material."

The conductor, like the public speaker, should have studied his material to the point where he, too, is in command of more to say than he will ever use.

Bruno Walter has said, "The dictionary of the conductor should be limited. The best word is *Espressivo.*" This should apply also to the hands of the conductor.

One occasionally hears the remark, "They pay too much attention to technique at the Conservatory." Nonsense! Perhaps a rephrasing might be better. Not "too much technique" but instead "too little artistry." Not "too much artistry" but "too little technique." *There is no such thing as too much technique or too much artistry.*

Editor's note: The following outline for score study is approximately that used in the classes in the Brussels Conservatory. A similar outline is used in Paris. It means seven trips through the score, with the knowledge and understanding increasing each time.

1. *Instrumentation and transpositions*
2. *Form analysis (large form, sonata, rondo, etc.)*
3. *Harmonic structure (especially analyzed where complicated)*
4. *Melodic line throughout and its instrumentation*
5. *Phrasal analysis (small phrases, minor structure)*
6. *Dynamics (dramatic climaxes, etc.)*
7. *Special effects in the score and manner of execution on the instruments (ponticello, muted passages, harmonics, etc.)*

Supplementary Readings *(See Appendix F)*

ADAM CARSE, *The Orchestra in the Eighteenth Century.*
RICHARD L. CROCKER, *A History of Musical Style.*
ROBERT A. MELCHER and WILLARD F. WARCH, *Music for Score Reading.*

---

[2] Doboujinsky was a Russian painter who worked a great deal in the theater, opera, and with the drama.

P. O. MORRIS and HOWARD FERGUSON, *Preparatory Exercises in Score Reading*.

PAUL STANTON, *The Dynamic Choral Conductor*, Chapter 8, "The Conductor's Attitude about Style and Repertoire."

Exercises for Practice (*Twenty Steps to Score-Study Facility*)

Use the Mahler, Dvořák, and Bach excerpts for this assignment, pages 140-55 in the Appendix. First, *mark the phrasing* in all three excerpts, as shown on pages 14-19 and explained on pages 37 and 38. Each excerpt is unique in the phrasing.* Then play through the following parts on the piano (or your major instrument), transposing to concert pitch. Do some of these every day. Stay with each problem until it becomes easy.

 1. Clarinets, pages 143-46.
 2. French Horns, page 140, upper stave; then lower stave.
 3. Trumpets, Mahler, pages 141-46, etc.
 4. Trombones, pages 142-43. Right octave?
 5. First with Second Violins, pages 150-55.
 6. Cellos, page 145-46.
 7. Violas, page 151-55. Right octave?
 8. Violin II with Viola, pages 151-55.
 9. Violin I with Cello, pages 147-49.
10. First Oboe with First Clarinet, pages 147-49.
11. Cello with First Bassoon, pages 147-49.
12. First and Second Horns with First and Second Trumpet, pages 36-37. The upper note in the Horns will sound an octave below the upper note in the trumpets.
13. Correlate the woodwind family, pages 147-49. Locate similarities or doublings before starting to play.
14. Correlate the brasses, page 140.
15. Correlate the Strings, pages 153-55.
16. Note the Percussion in Mahler, pages 142-46.
17. Play the melodic line throughout, skipping from instrument to instrument as the music changes. Decide which of the doubled parts is the most important. Pages 141-46, Mahler.
18. Read only the first note in each measure, starting with the basses and moving upward through the score until the flutes are reached. Pages 147-49.

19. Analyze the harmony on each beat in the Dvořák, pages 147-49.
20. Apply all of the above, except 5-9 and 15, to an assigned band score. Add some specialized exercises for the Saxophone parts.

* See page 156 for suggested phrasings.

chapter 4

Marking the Score

Malko

Editor's note: Just as Malko was an impeccable conductor technically so were his study scores edited in an impeccable manner. Professional conductors, glancing through his scores never cease to express admiration for the clarity of thought and the neatness of his markings. There is no mutilation of the notation. Each note is pristinely clear. Orchestral musicians (in a number of countries) who had played under Malko's direction invariably mention how easy he was to follow. His keenness of understanding coupled with a superbly masterful and fluently easy, knowledgeable manual technique, brought forth long-remembered musical results. After the Chicago appearance of the Copenhagen Symphony in 1952 when Malko conducted, the audience simply refused to go home. Encore followed encore, house lights were blinked and were finally completely extinguished before the audience could be persuaded to reach for its coats. One further word: Students studying with Malko were usually asked to edit one score with gestures. This was not intended to become a habit. Malko wanted only to know that the student understood when, where, and how to apply the technique. Such marking demonstrated the student's grasp of the scientific aspect of his work. It subtly required him to be conscious of the necessary technical skills as he studied the music itself.

There were and still are conductors who mark into the score the way or manner of conducting it. I was once told of the score of such a conductor. It had marks like this: "Attack the trombones violently." . . . "Look tenderly at the violins." . . . "Make a fist with the left hand." Needless to say I do not condone this practice.

Such a conductor was A. N. Vinogradsky. By profession he was a bank director; by avocation an amateur musician, but nevertheless a capable conductor. Great credit was due him in the development of the musical life of Kiev.

While conducting, Vinogradsky made faces and used his arms, hands, and whole body in an unscrupulously exhibitionistic way. One moment he would bend sideways as if permitting the melody of the cellos to flow past him into the audience. (It was in the first movement of the Kalinikoff First Symphony—he gave the first performance of this work.) Later, in the second theme, he "pulled" the thirds from the bassoons with the crooked finger of his left hand.

Vinogradsky was constantly inventing things to do. Although there were always underlying musical reasons for his inventions, 'they were, however, performed with an exaggeration barely short of clowning. He was once engaged to conduct a concert of the Russian Musical Society in St. Petersburg (Leningrad). (Vinogradsky was chairman of the Kiev branch.) Eduard Napravnik (the greatest of the "Russian" conductors of that time—he was born a Czech but stayed in Russia more than half a century and died there) was an invited guest to hear the concert. He told me, many years later, that the orchestra players of the Mariinsky Theater had said that Vinogradsky "guarded his scores most carefully and during the rehearsal breaks locked them into his music case." Once he forgot to turn the key and the musicians "of course" looked into his score. They found that all of his gestures and tricks were written down at the pertinent places showing a carefully and diligently prepared exhibitionism.

INTRODUCTION TO MARKING

Let us proceed now to the serious business of marking the score.

Neither scores nor players' parts should ever be marked in ink or indelible pencil because such marking eventually destroys the printed page since changes will inevitably be desirable from time to time (orchestra to orchestra and conductor to conductor).

Many publishers and libraries who lend music request that no marks be made in other than soft pencil which is easily erased. Unfortunately, people are careless. I have too often seen scores defaced with large handwriting that almost cut through the page—marks stressing *forte, piano, crescendo, ritenuto,* and so on. There are places where next to the printed ff or pp one finds as many as five markings repeating the same indications, made with different pencils (or even pen!) and showing various handwritings differing in size and slant. Why? Certainly there are dangerous places in most scores, and certainly these should be given special attention by the conductor. But is it necessary to deface the music to do so?

The markings made in the score are primarily for the purpose of learning the score. A student should be canny therefore in interpreting the marks left behind by the great conductors of the past. Such markings were, in general, made to grasp the musical content of the printed page during the score-study periods.

TWO KINDS OF SCORE MARKINGS

There are basically two kinds of score markings: (1) those that do not change the music but make the page easier to read and (2) those that do change the composer's written indications (dynamics for balance, corrections of mistakes, additions or changes in instrumentation, bowings, and so on).

Markings that Do Not Change the Score

Instrumentation   The first of the serviceable markings that do not change the score has to do with instrumentation. Customarily, all instruments needed for the performance of a composition are listed on the first page of the score. Thereafter when several instruments are not playing for a number of measures, their staves disappear from the printed page.

In many editions the name of each instrument, abbreviated, shows at the beginning of its score-line on each page. However, in some editions this needed help is missing, and it must be marked in by the conductor.

As an example let us quote from the Violin Concerto by Schoenberg, Op. 36. The music is extremely difficult and complicated. At certain places the early score showed only three or four lines and the instrumentation was missing. If we refer to the current G. Schirmer score which is now edited with the instrumentation, we find something like this (1939 printing, pages 78 and 79): On a split page the top line of the top half shows the first flute and first oboe; but the bottom half, on its top line, contains three trumpets *con sordino;* on the next page the top line holds the first, second, and fourth horns unmuted, and the lower half of the same page has the clarinets and bassoons on the top line. One can imagine the conductor's confusion over such an arrangement if the instrumentation is not indicated in the margin. In addition to such problems, the conductor is also dealing with tempo, rhythm, and a musical character that is incessantly changing. Obviously, the conductor would find it imperative to write in the instrumentation himself.

Often it is wise to indicate at the end of a page a change that occurs at the top of the next page.

Score lines are sometimes placed on the page so that the solo line is either higher or lower in position as page follows page. (Some conductor has marked a great upsweep of an arrow in thick black pencil!)

When the score page is divided into two parts so that it must be read twice (or sometimes several times), it is always practical to mark the division clearly in the margin as shown in Musical Example 4–1.

Musical Example 4–1: Tchaikovsky, *Francesca da Rimini*, measures 313–338.

*Malko's added markings. See also p. 43 in the text.

When the page is so crowded that there is barely room between the upper and lower halves of the score, one can mark, as Napravnik used to do, small pencil indications as shown in Diagram 4–A.

Diagram 4–A: Score-line separation marking.

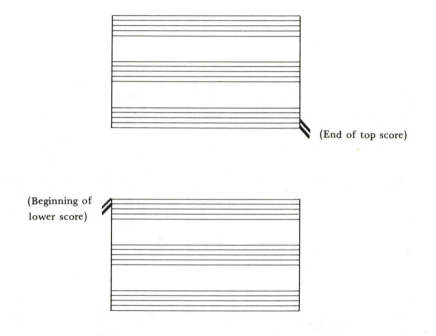

(End of top score)

(Beginning of lower score)

It should be done neatly. Unfortunately, conductors sometimes mark the margin in such a way that it is impossible to understand immediately what is meant.

One also sees at times the division of the score separated by a heavy blue or red line, straight across, or sometimes a wavy line. It is not easy to comprehend the reasoning behind these markings. They may be made to facilitate the reading of the score, but usually they distract instead. Because of such untidy and superfluous markings one cannot see the music itself. No wonder hostile feelings are sometimes generated!

Conductor Vyacheslav Suk came from Moscow for a guest appearance at the Mariinsky Theater in Leningrad. The opera to be performed was *Russlan and Ludmilla.* I saw him after a day or two of rehearsals. He remarked, "I spent the whole evening over the score of *Russlan.*"

"Why? Were you studying?"

"No! I worked the whole evening with an eraser."

"I know, I know—I have seen the score."

Another interesting anecdote in this connection: In Berlin Richard Strauss was invited to guest conduct Mozart's *Marriage of Figaro*. There was to be no rehearsal with the orchestra, only a runthrough with the piano. Fru Engle, the Danish singer who sang Suzanne, told this story. Everything was going well during the performance. Then, in the fourth act as she was singing her aria, she saw Strauss suddenly stop conducting, take something from his pocket, bend over the score, and start to work. The orchestra went on playing; she went on singing. In a moment Strauss diligently dusted off the score, put the eraser (!) back into his pocket and calmly (a little drowsy as always) resumed his conducting. Evidently the score had contained a *luft-pausa* or something *ad lib* inserted by another conductor and Strauss could not tolerate it.

Phrasing   Phrasing is the syntax of the score. Inefficiency is often seen in the markings of the punctuation of the phrase. Bars are seen numbered 1, 2, 3, and so on from the second or third measure of the period or even starting with the last bar of the phrase. Such marking belies the logical sense of the music and can only serve to confuse. Numbering measures phrasally is not predicated on mathematics. It is based only on a clear and intelligent deciphering of the phrasal content of the music (See Chart I, page 15).

There have been instances when the remark has been made, "Count the measures, memorize the number of measures, and you will be able to conduct the piece." Sorry to say, I cannot accept such a philosophy.

Counting measures and marking off phrases should be diligently, intelligently, and carefully done. *I consider phrasal analysis of the score to be an absolute necessity for the conductor.* In making this analysis he discovers many structural subtleties that might otherwise be overlooked, such as 3-, 5-, or 7-bar phrasal groupings. However, we should caution that, important as phrasal analysis is in score clarification, it should not stand alone and it should not be thought of as all-sufficient.

Phrasal markings may be indicated below the bottom line of the score. In Musical Example 4–2, notice the extension downward of the phrasal bar-line and indication of the number of measures in the *next* phrase to follow.

Musical Example 4–2: Brahms, Fourth Symphony, first movement, measures 317–330.

A phrase is "counted" orchestrally when a unit change occurs in the music. It may be the beginning of a new melody, the entrance of a new group of instruments, new rhythmic patterns, vital dynamic changes, harmonic sequences, and so on.

If the conductor wishes to remind himself of a certain sequence of phrases, he may mark the numerical sequence under the first measure of the series as shown in Musical Example 4–3.

* See p. 43.

Musical Example 4–3: Borodin, Second Symphony, first movement, measures 166 and following.

Editor's note: Refer to Chart I, page 15, and notice that Malko took into consideration the variance of phrasing between instruments in measures 122 to 141 of the chart.

In counting the phrase that is introduced by one or more up-beat notes at the end of a measure, the number one bar is the measure *following* the introductory notes, not the bar with the up-beat notes (Musical Example 4–4).

Musical Example 4–4: Wagner, Prelude to *Tristan and Isolde*, measures 36–42.

Editor's note: In Musical Example 4–4, notice the two-measure groupings as marked by Malko. The oboe echoes the phrase initiated by the violas; then the latter start the new phrase and the oboe again echoes. Observe the pitch of the entry-note each time. This is the clue to solving this sequence.

One occasionally encounters the problem of the interlocking phrase: a four-bar phrase ending on the first beat of the fourth bar, only to find the new phrase starting on that same beat. The composer has given the feeling for the four-measure phrase but has used only three full measures to do so. The conductor's attention should be given to the *entry of the new phrase* rather than the closing off of the old phrase. Mozart uses a similar device rather frequently (Musical Example 4–5).

Musical Example 4–5: Mozart, Così fan tutte Overture, measures 8–9.

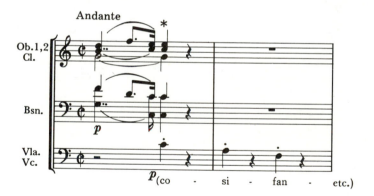

In Musical Example 4–6 we see the interlocking of the last note in the flute with the entrance of the violins—a dangerous place for the young conductor. The violins need their cue here.

Musical Example 4–6: Liszt, Les Preludes, measures 5–7.

Let us reiterate. Phrasal analysis is imperative as one step in building the broader musical concept of the composition as a whole.

Cues Certain editions and certain conductors indicate the important cues by large arrows pointing directly to the first note of the cue. This sometimes clutters up the score and tends to blot out the notes themselves.

I have made it a practice to mark the abbreviation for the cued instrument directly above the entry beat in the *top margin* of the score. Again, black pencil is used. Refer to the top margin of Musical Example 4–4.

When two or more instruments enter at the same time, customarily the one having the greatest musical importance (such as the main theme) is placed highest in the margin, with the others following either in order of musical importance or in score order below it. In this way the eye catches instantly the entrance and the relationship of the several instruments. The need to search down through the score is eliminated. This device is especially helpful when rehearsing *à livre ouvert* (open score on the stand), and is a definite timesaver in the rehearsal.

Dynamics We have alluded to the addition of repetitive markings of *forte* and *piano* in scores conducted by different conductors. When Albert Coates came to the Mariinsky Theater to conduct his compositions, he had marked the *fortes* and *pianos* by encircling them. I do not know if it was his invention or not, but in any case it does make it easier for the eyes and it keeps the page clean. I myself vary this marking by using a red pencil for the *forte* and blue for the *piano*.

The sf's are marked with half circles in red thus: (sf) The forte-pianos are also marked with half circles, red on the forte side and blue on the piano: red (fp) blue.

Crescendos may be underlined where necessary with red, diminuendos with blue. Such marks, carefully made and not touching anything else can be very useful. And they are more practical than the huge scribbling of extra *crescendo* and *piano* markings defacing the music.

When there are sequential entrances, instrument to instrument, they may be shown as given in Musical Example 4–7.

Musical Example 4–7: Borodin, Second Symphony, finale, measures 92–94.

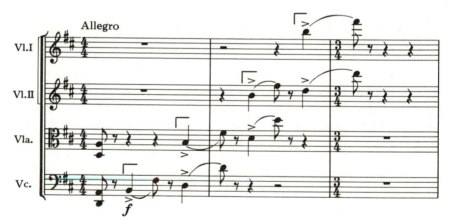

The indicating "bracket" is done in red or blue to show simultaneously the dynamic.

Editor's note: In the given example the brackets were marked in red and Malko had marked the passage poco sostenuto *in black pencil.*

Dangerous Places in the Score   Almost every score contains problems for the conductor, dangerous places where the attention of the conductor must be well focused if the performance is to come off effectively and efficiently. It is good to have a special marking for such places. This mark will alert the mind during the study periods and remind the conductor of the danger when he picks up the score months later. The *nota bene* ("note it well!") can be condensed into the following sign: NB See Musical Example 4–2, below the seventh measure, and also Musical Example 4–4, top of the page.

Marks that Change the Score

We might say that marks that do not change the score are for the conductor's eyes and those that do change the score are for the ears. Under the latter category may be classified such markings as the addition or subtraction of instrumentation, the adjustment of dynamics in order to balance the music for a certain orchestra or a certain concert hall, the correction of mistakes in the score and parts, and bowings.

Change of Instrumentation   Changes in instrumentation have much to do with the historical development of the orchestra and particularly the perfecting of the wind instruments mechanically. In Beethoven's day certain notes were not playable on some of the wind instruments at his disposal. For example, in his Seventh Symphony, first movement, the trumpets are dropped out in measures 125 and 127, leaving the dominant harmony incomplete in the brass; and in measure 132 the second horn has to jump twelve notes (to high D from G below the staff) because the low D was not playable. There are many such discrepancies in music of that period. On today's instruments all notes are playable so that in current renditions the missing notes are usually written into the score and parts.

The doubling or deletion of like instruments is not a fundamental change in the composer's ideas. With the large string sections in the modern orchestra very often the woodwind parts have to be doubled for effective balance. This may be indicated in the score by marking a capital letter D next to the winds to be doubled. Doubling of intensity is not a question of principle. If two horns make a passage sound better than one horn, then two should be used (Musical Examples 4–8 and 4–9).

Musical Example 4–8: Beethoven, Seventh Symphony, third movement, measures 181–182.

Musical Example 4–9: Beethoven, *Leonore* Overture, No. 3, measures 524–528 (as shown in the score).

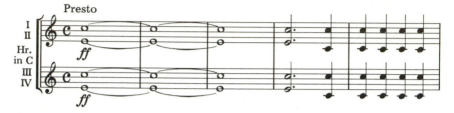

Editor's note: Here Malko adds this notation which may be of interest since it is an example of his thorough knowledge and thorough research in the building of his interpretations: "Beethoven, Seventh Symphony, end of second movement. Compare with the String Quartet, Op. 130, small score, pages 23 and 25. All instruments pizzicato except the first violin which is arco."

Similarly, deleting of like instruments is not a change in the composition itself, although it is a change in the notation. If the volume of sound must diminish in certain instruments with a given orchestra, it may be necessary to undouble the parts or to drop out half of the string section. In Musical Example 4–10 we find certain doublings that may have to be adjusted for continuity of dynamic.

Musical Example 4–10: Wagner, *Tannhauser* Overture, measures 273–274 and 277–278.

In Musical Example 4–11 the oboes can be deleted.

Musical Example 4–11: von Weber, *Der Freischütz* Overture, measures 251–253.

In Musical Example 4–12, beginning with measure 157 and continuing for ten measures, the composer's request for the *leggiero* is often enhanced by dropping out half of the first and second violins.

Musical Example 4–12: Brahms, Fourth Symphony, first movement, measures 157–160.

An interesting adjustment is seen in Musical Example 4–13. The power of the first violins should increase during this passage. The individual trepidation is lost if they are leveled off with the first flute and first oboe. Therefore, in measures 100 and 101 it is advantageous to have the first violins play *divisi* at the octave, adding the upper notes in measure 100 and adjusting accordingly in measure 101. Following this, in measure 102, the use of the G string is recommended as the first violins emerge.

Musical Example 4–13: Brahms, Fourth Symphony, second movement, measures 98–102.

In Beethoven's Seventh Symphony, first movement, the second violins are often omitted by the conductor in measures 205 and 206 because they do not appear in the parallel passage (measures 211 and 212). However, omitting the second violins takes out the bass note (G) of the harmony so the horns, sounding the upper G, are then required to play *divisi* at the lower octave to cover this omission (Musical Example 4–14).

Musical Example 4–14: Beethoven, Seventh Symphony, first movement, measures 205–206.

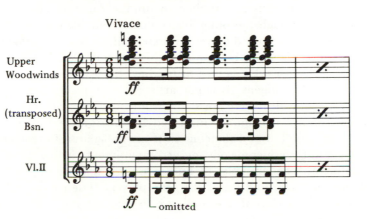

Adjusting the Dynamics   It may be said that the conductor has more leeway in the field of dynamics than in any other command in the score. Dynamics are subtle and adjustable. Fine musical sensitivity is important in their handling.

In this connection let us mention immediately the controversial first note in measures 228 and 240 of Beethoven's Fifth Symphony, first movement. Some editions show p or pp while others show f or ff (Musical Example 4–15). (The ff is preferable.)

Musical Example 4–15: Beethoven, Fifth Symphony, first movement, measures 228–229.

There are two kinds of dynamics orchestrally: (1) the general musical directive applicable to the tutti orchestra and (2) the dynamic necessary to the individual instrument within the tutti orchestra. The conductor as well as the player must understand the individuality of the various instruments and their own unique function and possibility for projection through the other instruments—and likewise their ability to retire modestly within the over-all orchestral sound. No composer can ideally balance his score. He can state his general idea, but player and conductor have to work together to produce the score in the fullness of its beauty by intelligent dynamic artistry. The things the composer wrote must sound—if it were not so, he would not have written them.

An orchestral dynamic as indicated by the composer is a dynamic of *resultant* sound. But balancing instrument against instrument, and melody against counter-melody or accompaniment, is the province of the conductor. The subtleties of fine orchestral balance depend on the ear of the conductor and the skill of the players. The conductor's job is to make the score clear to the audience so that the music the composer had in mind is intelligible to the ears of the listeners.

A change in dynamic relationship among instruments is always permissible if it clarifies the ideas of the composer and makes the performance more understandable and enjoyable for the audience. Requiring special attention from the conductor is the balancing of melody line against sustained tones marked *forte* or *double-forte*. In Musical Example 4–16, if the brasses play triple *forte* as notated, nothing will be heard from the strings who are the real center of interest at this moment.

Musical Example 4–16: Dvorak, Fifth Symphony, first movement, measures 41–39 from the end.

It is necessary in Musical Example 4–16 to highlight the first and second violins, to bring them forward through the mass of sound. This is done by dropping back the brasses to a single *forte* immediately after their ff attack. Thereafter the intense *double-forte* of the whole string section will guarantee that this passage will not be heard only as a *mezzo-forte*.

Editor's note: Recently a French horn player from the Chicago Symphony was heard to remark, "Reiner would never permit us to hold out a sustained note at its full double-forte *dynamic against a melody line. We always had to drop back after attacking it at its written level."*

Richard Strauss likewise was conscious of the same principle since he applied it judiciously in the fourth movement of Mozart's Jupiter Symphony, K 551. Also, in the first movement, measures 147–148, he writes, "The theme should be ff instead of *forte* for the violas, cellos and basses." (The full outline of the Strauss editing for this movement is given at the end of this chapter.)

We should not leave the subject of dynamic adjustment without calling attention to the variation of dynamics for musical effect, the subtleties of performance not written by the composer. These have to rely on the musicianship of the performers. One example should suffice (Musical Example 4–17).

Musical Example 4–17: Mozart, Symphony in C Major, K 551, first movement, measures 98–100.

In this example, the violins must emerge at a dynamic louder than the written *piano* and then *diminuendo* down to the required dynamic. If they play an immediate *piano,* as notated, *they are not heard by the audience for several notes.* The fp occurs *automatically* when the full orchestra drops out.

The aim of such subtleties, added by the conductor, is to explain and deepen the musical sense of the score. Great care should be taken not to rewrite the composer's musical ideas. It is one thing to adjust a dynamic to give the composer the sound he intended, but it is quite another thing to restate his ideas by substituting *crescendos* for sudden *fortes, diminuendos* for *piano-subitos,* sustained *fortes* for *sforzato* accents and so on.

Correcting Misprints and Composer's Errors   Proofreading orchestra parts against the score is very important. To spend valuable rehearsal time finding and correcting errors in the parts is a waste of time and effort. This should be done beforehand by a competent proofreader.

Today there are far fewer mistakes in printed music than formerly, but errors still do creep in. Sometimes the composer himself is responsible, sometimes the publisher.

Musical Example 4–18: Schubert, Seventh Symphony, fourth movement, measures 165–170 and 753–757.

First time (165–170)

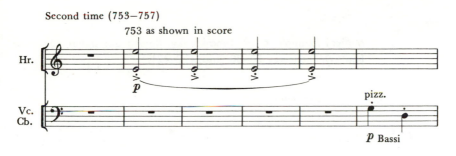

Second time (753–757)

753 as shown in score

Hr.

p

pizz.

Vc.
Cb.

p Bassi

There is an incident connected with Rachmaninoff's performance of his piano concerto with the Chicago Symphony Orchestra. In the rehearsal he stopped the orchestra and said, "First clarinet, not F-natural but F-sharp." Then, to himself but so that everyone could hear, "It is my fault."

Glazounov thought that in Schubert's Seventh Symphony, fourth movement, measures 753–756, the horn should be G, not E, for four bars as printed. The G would make it analogous to the first passage, measures 165–168 (Musical Example 4–18).

The attitudes of conductors toward misprints are varied. Sir Henry Wood, hearing a mistake at rehearsal, would try to find what the chord was and search into its logic. Sir Thomas Beecham would say, "What is it? F-sharp? Play F-natural. Try E-flat. . . . Play it pp!"

It can happen that a symphony or opera may be performed for many years with undiscovered mistakes. Vyacheslav Suk found a misprint in *Aida* when he conducted it in Moscow. Toscanini likewise discovered an error in one of the older operas. Felix Mottl, in St. Petersburg, told the bass clarinet in the Vorspiel to *Lohengrin* to play an octave higher than the part was usually played. There was at that time still some confusion as to the manner of notation for the bass clarinet. I myself have seen two scores for the *Lohengrin* Introduction where the notation differed: In one case the bass clarinet was written a ninth higher than the actual sound; in the other, a second higher.

The same confusion is found in parts for the celli when they are written in the treble clef. Sometimes they appear an octave higher than the actual sound, as in *Romeo and Juliet* by Tchaikovsky, measures 78 and 419 and the following; and sometimes they sound as written (Musical Example 4–19).

Musical Example 4–19: Tchaikovsky, *Romeo and Juliet,* Overture Fantasy, measures 78–80 and 419–421.

In Verdi's Requiem, at the beginning of number 3, the Offertoire, in the second bar the celli sound as notated in the treble clef, but from the thirteenth bar onward they sound an octave lower. Why?

Sometimes mistakes are played when they do not actually occur in the score. A famous example concerns Toscanini's days as cellist in the opera in Brazil. The conductor stopped in rehearsal and reprimanded Toscanini:

"Why don't you play your part correctly?"

"?"

"You played it differently yesterday."

"Oh, yes! At that rehearsal I was playing the first violin passages."

It was during this same tour that Toscanini started his career as a conductor, taking over unexpectedly the performance of *Aida.*

Orchestra players have a passion for stories connected with mistakes in the parts. Often their stories are greatly exaggerated. Such an experience was mine when I arrived in Amsterdam and found out, at the airport, that my rehearsal for *Lohengrin* was due in an hour. I had understood that the rehearsals were to take place the following day in Hilversum. Unfortunately, my rehearsal glasses were in my luggage and there was nothing I could do to get them for the Amsterdam rehearsal. The next day, arriving in Hilversum, the radio sound director told me "All Holland knows about it."

"About what?"

"Yesterday you found a misprint in the horn part for the *Lohengrin!*"

Personally, I still think there was no misprint, but instead that the horn player had just made a mistake in his performance and did not grasp immediately what had happened. But the story grew out of all proportion to the incident.

The ear of the conductor, as well as that of the player, has an intimate connection with the discovery of wrong notes and misstated rhythms. I have found, even in the conductor's score, upon many occasions, misprints. In one edition of *Boris Godounov* I found more than forty mistakes. In some of the other editions there were not so many.

Once in *Ladoiska* by Cherubini I was quite at a loss. It was a wonderful old edition in which each page reminded one of a beautiful antique engraving. There was a tremendous number of mistakes—all of a rather elementary character. I asked the musicologist-composer Felix Borowski (Chicago) about it. He said, "It is always like that in the old scores." I pointed to a spot that was troubling me. Borowski explained, "A simple modulation and everything is clear—the composer just did not mark the sharp for the note F in any of the voices. It is clear without it!" (!) Well, one never ceases to learn.

In the *Queen of Spades* by Tchaikovsky, second scene, Pauline sings, "Look, I shall complain to the prince about you." There is a famous D-natural that used to confuse conductors and they would cancel it out. B. Khaikin (Moscow) wrote me that when he rehearsed it in the Opera Theater of Stanislavsky, Conductor Suk "stood behind my back eagerly awaiting what would come, D-natural or D-flat."

Sometimes there are legally accepted mistakes in the score. For example, in the *William Tell* Overture by Rossini, when the English horn returns to the reprise (Andante, 3/8, 33rd bar), the last note is played concert pitch A, written pitch E. In the original score it is notated F-sharp, sounding B-natural (Musical Example 4–20).

Editor's note: The correction appears in some of the current editions.

Musical Example 4–20: Rossini, *William Tell* Overture, andante section, bar 33.

In general the editions of the Rossini Overtures would make an excellent subject for intensive study by a musicologist.

In Beethoven's *Fifth Symphony,* second movement, *Andante con moto,* measures 224–225, all editions show the bassoons as given in Musical Example 4–21.

Musical Example 4–21: Beethoven, Fifth Symphony, second movement, measures 224–225.

But in Beethoven's manuscript (according to musicologist G. Jonas) these notes do not appear. This strange fact may be accounted for in that in Beethoven's day there were few violas. Those that were in the orchestra may have sounded too weak and somebody reinforced them by adding the bassoons, even changing certain passages. However, in our modern orchestras, the passage sounds better without the bassoons.

Eric Kleiber [1] showed me a photostat of some pages from Beethoven's *Seventh Symphony.* In the first movement (bar 300, second *fermata*) the winds have a *piano* marking. The strings have no such sign and Kleiber insisted that Beethoven did it on purpose—the strings playing *double-forte.* This I doubt. In Beethoven's day they used fewer strings and this probably accounts for Beethoven's omission of the *piano* in the string parts. It is likewise possible that the difference between a *piano* and a *forte* rendition of the *pizzicato* was negligible. In bar 301 (arco) the *piano* marking appears. However, to interpret the strings today as *double-forte* on the *piano-fermata* would be illogical.

Still more interesting is a spot in the second movement of the *Seventh Symphony*—the dynamics of the second theme (bars 102–139 and 225–242, coda). In all editions there are *crescendos* and *diminuendos* in these places. In the manuscript, Beethoven shows only the *diminuendos* the second time. This *diminuendo* without the *crescendo* lends a special charm to the passage. Musical Example 4–22 will locate the passage.

Editor's note: *If the reader does not have the score immediately available, we should explain that the passage starting in bar 102 is a lengthy one, continuing for some 37 measures and leading eventually*

---

[1] Eric Kleiber (1890–1956) was the Berlin State Opera Conductor in 1923 and for some years thereafter. He left Germany in 1935 and settled in South America.

after the last diminuendo to piano, *to a* crescendo *and* fortissimo *climax. The second time (bar 225 and following) there are only eighteen measures which lead to a* pianissimo *entrance of the first theme in the winds against* pianissimo *sustained notes in the strings, a very different topography (Musical Example 4–22).*

Musical Example 4–22: Beethoven, Seventh Symphony, second movement, measures 110–115.

As examples of miswriting by the composers themselves the following are pertinent: In the *Oberon* Overture by von Weber, measure 22, the *caesura* is not printed in the right place. Musical Example 4–23 shows it (a) as written and (b) as it should be written.

Musical Example 4–23: von Weber, Oberon Overture, measure 22.

At the end of *Der Freischütz* Overture (von Weber) a similar incorrect notation is seen. The *fermata* should occur (does occur in perfor-

mance!) on the half rest. Then the eighth rest is given in the baton for
the music to continue. Musical Example 4–24 shows it (a) as notated and
(b) as corrected.

Musical Example 4–24: von Weber, *Der Freischütz* Overture,
measures 282–283.

(a) As notated by composer

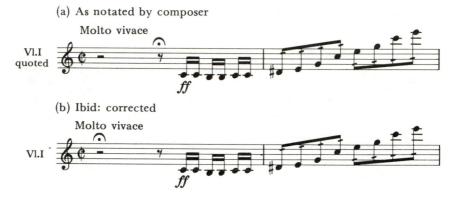

(b) Ibid: corrected

Retouches   And now we come to the retouching of the score, the
"improvements" and actual changes the conductor sometimes makes.
This is a special theme and not a simple one. The slight changes a conductor may insert for a "creative performance" should be handled with
extreme caution.

Nikisch, in the Tchaikovsky Fourth Symphony, last eleven bars,
inserted a *piano-subito*. In the Beethoven Seventh, Finale, the *piano-
subito* occurred twice.

Retouches often have to do with the striving for a more effective
ending. The following have been used in the specified places:

Dvorak: *Symphony No. Five,* last bar—not *diminuendo* but ff.

Schubert: *Symphony No. Seven,* end of the Finale: It is marked
diminuendo, but sometimes the conductors do not observe it.

von Weber: *Der Freischütz* Overture, starting with bar 292, Nikisch
would start pp, then *crescendo*. In his time it produced a fine effect, but
is it necessary now?

Wagner: *Tannhauser*—the counterpoint at the end. Nikisch almost
reorchestrated it, adding, crossing out, changing to eight, increasing instruments, changing slurs, dynamics, editing doublings in woodwinds
and horns, and so on. All of his work added to the suspense of the performance.

There are certain places in many scores where the composer himself did some rewriting, for example, the cuts made by Mozart in the Haffner Symphony and his reworking of the *Serenade.*

Debussy made retouches in his tone poem *La Mer:* pages 18, 19, 86, 89, 97, 98, 100, 104, 107, 116, 121, 125, 126, 134, 136, and other places (Edition A. Durand & Fils, Paris, 1905).

Liszt and Toscanini both did some retouching in *Les Preludes.*

In the current editions, many of the retouches are now in print, especially in the large new editions. It is unfortunate that these changes are not stipulated in the forewords where pertinent.

According to Horowitz, Toscanini changed many things, for example, individual notes, ornaments, and so on, explaining why it should be done. For the *melisme—*ornaments, *appoggiaturas, acciaccaturas, mordants, vorschlags—*ready recipes there are none. No really reliable formula exists.

Editor's note: *Pay attention to the upside-down* mordant *in Wagner's* Rienzi *Overture.*

Retouches occur within the body of a work to create more suspense, greater climaxes, or more subtle emotional effects.

In the *Oberon* Overture by von Weber, the following retouches are frequently heard: A *caesura* and pause before the last two sixteenth notes in bar 182 (Musical Example 4–25).

Musical Example 4–25: von Weber, Oberon Overture, measure 182.

In measure 55, instead of the fp in the horn, the entrance is made *piano* followed by a *crescendo.* The second time, in bar 58 it is sufficient just to press on the *piano* a bit (Musical Example 4–26).

Musical Example 4–26: von Weber, Oberon Overture, measures 54–60.

(as shown in the score)

Editor's note: *In measures 117–119 the passages in the strings are started up-bow, and the up-down sequence continues throughout the scale. This is one of the very few places in the entire repertoire when a succession of sixteenth notes is played "standing on its head." Generally, a series of unslurred sixteenths on consecutive beats is played with the down-bow falling on the first note in each beat (Musical Example 4–27).*

Musical Example 4–27: von Weber, Oberon Overture, measures 117–119.

Nikisch doubled the horns and brought out the woodwind passage in measures 209–212 (Musical Example 4–28).

Musical Example 4–28: von Weber, *Oberon* Overture, measures 209–212.

In *Petrushka* (Stravinsky), Nikisch changed page 125 and he actually reorchestrated the first scene in *Le Sacre du Printemps*. He also inserted a cut in the second movement of Schubert's Seventh Symphony.

In the Tchaikovsky Sixth Symphony, first movement, the bass clarinet is usually substituted for the bassoon as shown in Musical Example 4–29. This is acceptable and understandable.

Musical Example 4–29: Tchaikovsky, Sixth Symphony, first movement, measures 148–160.

Mahler made many changes in the symphonies of Schumann. There is not a single page that does not show changes of some sort.

Editor's note: *Pages 1 and 12 of the first movement of the Fourth Symphony and the last movement on page 124 are mentioned but not specified.*

The Beethoven Seventh Symphony opens with the fp chord, the oboe emerging therefrom, piano, with the melody line. A good way to handle this is to suggest that the oboe ignore the *forte* and simply play *piano* throughout. Mahler used the *piano* here: "Nobody will hear it and it is more practical from the standpoint of the oboist."

Mahler did a magnificent editing of the Beethoven Seventh Symphony. I obtained a manuscript copy from the librarian of the Czech Philharmonic Orchestra. One page is reproduced here in full, showing Mahler's editing, contrasted with Beethoven's original (Musical Examples 4–30 and 4–31).

Musical Example 4–30: Beethoven, Seventh Symphony, *(Mahler editing)*, first movement, measures 242–254.

Musical Example 4–31: Beethoven, Seventh Symphony (original),
measures 241–254.

* In the original each part except the flute is marked *cresc. poco a poco* with a
dotted line leading to the ff in measure 254.

(Beethoven original)

(Beethoven original)

Editor's note: Mahler edited all of the Beethoven symphonies, but these editions are generally no longer available.

Some conductors create inventions—the idea of a dialogue between instruments.

Absurdities   From time to time one finds editings that have no apparent logic for their existence. Among these may be quoted the following.

Beethoven, Piano Concerto No. 5 in E-flat: In Prague, on page 70 of the score, the French horns were substituted for the triplets in the violas. Again on page 71 the horns replaced the second violins (measures 181 and 186–187).

And then there was the measure that someone had crossed out in score and parts in the Beethoven Fifth Symphony! I think it was in Kharkov, page 21, fourth bar.

Editor's note: We cannot identify this place conclusively.

Coates reshuffled the movements in Rachmaninoff's *The Bells*. I cannot endorse musically what happened. It would appear that in this case the whole is not equal to the sum of the parts. In music the sum changes when the parts are reshuffled.

Bowings   Uniformity of bowing throughout the string section is best on tutti passages. It gives the rendition a more unified interpretation. An identical passage played by different sections with different bowing can give the effect of two interpretations proceeding concurrently. However, cellos and basses are allowed some leeway, especially if the passage bristles with string-crossings.

Toscanini paid very little attention to bowings. "Naturale" was his exhortation and this applied not only to bowings but also to the breathing of the chorus. This naturalness is correct.

Frederick Stock (Chicago Symphony) paid a great deal of attention to the bowing. (He had been a viola player in the orchestra for some years before assuming the conductorship.)

Rimsky-Korsakoff used to say, "If you do not play a stringed instrument, whistle to decide the bowing." His meaning was that a feeling of breathing in would result in an up-bow marking and breathing out, a down-bow.

The old Russian orchestras stressed a large sweep of the bow. The Germans, on the other hand, were economical in the use of the bow.

The personality of each orchestra influences and is influenced by the bowings they use. The same is true of the chorus in its manner of breathing. In the orchestra the concertmaster recognizes and deals with the orchestra's personality through his choice of bowings. When the composer's bowings are artificial rather than natural, the concertmaster will invent certain finesses to make the execution of the music both easy and natural.

One finds many passages in which the composer's slurs signify phrasing rather than bowing, for example, the Prelude to the first act of *Lohengrin* by Wagner in which the slur covers a number of measures, making it impossible to execute the passage without change of bow direction. One must distinguish between the phrasing slur and the bowing slur. In *Lohengrin,* the composer's intention was to request a perfectly smooth legato and utter poise in the motion. Such markings place the logic of the music above the logic of the execution. To handle such passages, the musicians subtly agree to change bow direction not simultaneously but a moment apart. In this way the smoothness is preserved.

The individuality of the particular orchestra should be taken into consideration by the conductor in his choice of bowings.

Hans Lange (Chicago Symphony) mentioned the emphasis as falling generally on the odd-numbered measures as contrasted with the less emphatic even-numbered measures. The down-bow would then correspond to the heavier accented measures.

Klemperer, in Leningrad, conducting Mozart's G-minor Symphony, K 550, with bowing by Rose, permitted the bowing shown in Musical Example 4–32 (a), upper bowing, starting at the frog.

This bowing belies the musical sense of the passage—and how often we see such bowings!

Musical Example 4–32: Mozart, Symphony in G Minor, K 550, opening measures.

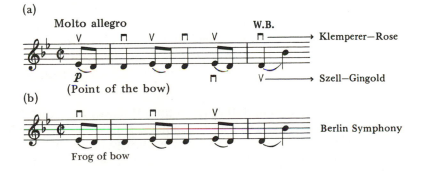

(a)

Molto allegro   W.B.

Klemperer—Rose

p
(Point of the bow)

Szell—Gingold

(b)

Berlin Symphony

Frog of bow

Editor's note: The Cleveland Symphony under George Szell also used this bowing but starting at the point of the bow with a legato effect. Szell wanted to produce the longer two-bar phrase as a unit, unbroken by the bowing articulations. The Berlin Philharmonic, on the other hand, uses the "traditional" bowing, starting down-bow at the frog and articulating the two-note groupings as Mozart wrote them. This is the more accepted bowing (Musical Example 4–32(b)).

The first note of the *Coriolanus* Overture by Beethoven is played with the spelled bowing, no two players changing the direction of the bow at the same moment. In the Fifth Symphony (Beethoven), von Bulow used a combination of *divisi*, half the violins sustaining the slur as written and the other half changing the bow to preserve the sound (second movement, measure 110 and following). The same in the *Leonore No. 3*.

The following incident was related by a Mr. Zweig in Prague, December 3, 1937:

Once Otto Klemperer played the *Suite No. 3* by Bach exactly as written in the original, without dynamics, without bowings. Zemlinsky did not approve, but he did acknowledge "still it was some kind of a performance."

Editor's note: A similar occurrence concerns the Messiah by Handel: A former concertmaster had spent much time and thought correlating and marking the bowing among the several string sections for the annual performance of this music. Sometime after he had left the orchestra it was decided, for the sake of variety, to change the format of the annual performance and to give a "new" rendition using the score in its original writing, without bowings, with harpsichord, and so on. The customary conductor officiated on all occasions. The former concertmaster went to the performance. He later described it as the least coordinated, least inspired performance he had ever heard. The audience reaction was also unfavorable although they could not pinpoint why. Using the original, unedited bowings, the unnaturalness is immediately noticeable. One has to remember that orchestral bowings had not been "solved" in the days of Bach and Handel. Accentuation now customarily has to fall on the down-bow. The music loses its natural rhythmic drive when this "law of nature" is denied.

Finally, let us remark that the technical marks for indicating certain conductorial gestures are few in number, but these few do deserve a right to exist. They are a more positive contribution to the score and its subsequent rendition than the many and various careless markings one so often finds, markings repeating only the already indicated directions of the composer. Repetitious markings, by reason of their existence, reveal a lack of conscientious memorizing of the composer's written directives.

To close this chapter we give Richard Strauss' notes as they appear in the score of Mozart's Jupiter Symphony, K 551, the first movement. These notes stress the attention necessary to the production of the finest possible rendition of any score. Of the many markings we may find one or two that seem formally to contradict the score, but after close analysis we see that there is no such contradiction. They show only a more accurate delineation of the composer's written intentions. Such adjustments have to do with the physical sound of the orchestra itself in relation to the efficiency of the human ear.

RICHARD STRAUSS' EDITING OF THE MOZART SYMPHONY IN C MAJOR (JUPITER) K 551, FIRST MOVEMENT

The history of these notes is as follows: Richard Strauss conducted this symphony with a European orchestra in 1916 (?). The librarian of this orchestra made a copy of these notes and gave it to me in 1932. These markings point out the performing-rendition ideas of Strauss who was famous for his superior classical interpretations of Mozart's works.

Here are the notes:

Editor's note: *Malko's observations appear in parenthesis.*

Bar 3: First violins. (Note the tenuto mark over the first note in the measure.)

Bar 4: All strings have the diminuendo sign: ▬▬▬▬▬
Bars 7–8: The same (a natural dynamic espressivo).
Bars 26–27: First and second violins, the same.
Bar 30: Again the same tenuto sign as in bar 3, followed by a crescendo:

(In bars 3, 32, 33, 34, there is no indication of diminuendo but logically and by analogy with the preceding example the diminuendo is natural. See bar 4.)

Bar 35: Crescendo for the first and second violins, not for two bars, but only for the first bar. (This can be interpreted either as a crescendo leading to forte (bar 37), or espressivo for these two bars without any emphasis on the *subito forte*. For me this second possibility is obvious.)

(c)

Bars 56–57:   (d)

The same in bars 58–59 for the violas, cellos, and basses.

Bar 58: Grazioso for the first violins.

Bar 60: Pp for the violas, cellos, basses.

(e)

Bar 61: First violins.

(f)

Bar 77: Before the second note, pp for violas, cellos, and basses.

(g)

Bar 78: Diminuendo before the second note for all strings.

Bar 79: Before the first note, pp for the first and second violins, with ppp for the violas, cellos and basses.

(h)

Bar 99: Instead of the piano, use it as marked:

(This last example is one of the rare occasions where it looks as if Strauss had changed the composer's intention. However, the result will be nearer Mozart's idea by preserving the espressivo to the end of the phrase.)

Bar 107: Crescendo for the whole bar, first and second violins.

Bar 108: 110 (?): Diminuendo on the second half of the first bar, first and second violins.

Bar 119: Crescendo for the whole bar, first and second violins.

Bar 121: Tranquillo for the flute, oboe, and bassoon.

Bars 126–127: First and second violins crescendo.

Bars 129–130: Crescendo-diminuendo for violins 1 and 2. (The same as 107, 108.)

Bars 131–132: The same for oboe and bassoon.

Bar 147: Double forte for violas, cellos, basses. (The same as 107, 108.)

Bar 153: Violin I not *piano* but diminuendo into bar 154 where the *piano* materializes.

notated: *p*

(This example, bar 153, again might seem as if the composer's intention had been denied. Compare with bar 99. In actual fact, however, the listener will hear just what the composer intended. Compare this with the *pp subito* of the cellos and basses in the introduction to the Seventh Symphony of Beethoven:

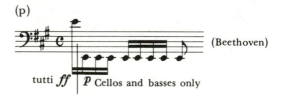

tutti *ff*   *p* Cellos and basses only   (Beethoven)

(Gustav Mahler said, "Play the second note not pp but mf, third note mp, then p and pp. Then the listener will hear what the composer wrote.")

Bars 159–160: Crescendo-diminuendo.

Bar 161: Pp instead of p for all strings.

Bar 162: The last note of the first and second violins, *piano* (see preceding example).

Bar 164: Diminuendo for the first and second violins (same as bar 30).

Bars 191–192 and 195–196: Like bars 3–4.

Bars 214–215: The same as above.

Bars 218–219: Like bars 30–31.

Bar 244 and the following: Like bar 56 and the measures following it. However, bar 249 is not marked the same as before:

(In bar 61, the first violins have the crescendo mark for the whole bar. Here the second half of the measure, marked diminuendo, is probably done this way in order to let the flute and bassoon through.)

Bars 265–267: Analogous to bar 99.

Bar 305: Crescendo for the whole bar with the whole orchestra except the flute which has the crescendo in the last half of the bar.

Bar 306: Ff for the whole orchestra.

Bars 309–310: Crescendo for the horns and trumpets and timpani.

Bar 311: Ff for the same instruments.

Supplementary Readings (*See Appendix F*)

E. A. H. GREEN, *Orchestral Bowings and Routines,* first four chapters.

EMIL KAHN, *Handbook for Conducting.* Edited scores are therein for a number of works.

GARDNER READ, *Thesaurus of Orchestral Devices.*

Exercises for Practice *(Marking the Score)*

Edit fully the scores on pages 141-55 using the steps outlined below. If you have not already done so, mark the phrasing first.

1. Where instrumentation is missing in the left margin, write it in.
2. Using red and blue pencils, encircle the *fortes* in red, the *pianos* in blue. When all parts have the same printed dynamic, it is sufficient to mark only the top line and the first violin part. Mark the *sf* and *fp* as given on page 42.
3. Edit the most important entrances (melodic) using a bracket thus:
   The red or blue designation is helpful here, too.
4. Notate all necessary cues at the top of the page, directly above the entrance beat. Abbreviate the instrument designation. Use black pencil for this.
5. If there are dangerous spots where the conductor must be very alert, use the NB, *nota bene,* mark. Place it in the top or bottom margin.

5

Imagination, Interpretation,

and Memorization

Green

One never ceases to marvel at the complexities and awesome wonder of the human mind: its ability to work on two levels, so to speak —the factual or mechanical and the non-factual or artistic.

Chapter 1 dealt with the improvement of pitch imagination, a "mechanic" of score study. Interpretation, however, deals with the use of the imagination on its creative or artistic plane.

The memory, too, has its bi-level aspects. Malko termed them the "analytical" and the "spontaneous." The former is an intense concentration on remembering what is analyzed during the score-study hours. The latter is the "free-wheeling" or "subconscious" acquisition of knowledge such as occurs when an often-heard melody can be reproduced without conscious effort.

Let us now consider interpretative imagination.

INTERPRETATIVE IMAGINATION

Interpretative imagination deals with the inspirational profile of the music, its emotional content, its personalized appeal. Joy, sorrow, peace and calm, turbulence and excitement, nobility, gentleness, triumph or despair—they are all there. And it is the province of the interpreter, the conductor, to ferret out from the marks on the page the real meaning that lies behind them. Richard Wagner called it the *melos*.

No piece of great music has endured without its emotional undercurrent. Also, no piece of great music remains static, measure after measure, on one plane of emotional intensity. The conductor's sensitivity to the subtleties eventuates in his interpretation. The interpretative imagination takes over and finally comes into focus during the rehearsals and subsequent performances.

Needless to say, the resulting rendition of the music should be logical and consistent, as well as musically inspirational. And the composer's directives should not be ignored.

On the down-to-earth, practical side, for example, a too sudden *sforzato* in a passage of calm can break the mood. An overlooked *fermata,* denying its extra length and thus negating an emotional climax, leaves the audience less than inspired. An indicated *triple-piano,* played with an indifferent *mezzo-forte,* is an unforgivable tragedy of the first magnitude. Only the conductor's musicianship, coupled with his interpretative imagination, can prevent such sorry occurrences. They are his responsibility.

APPLYING INTERPRETATIVE IMAGINATION

One sometimes wonders just how much "training" can be given to something as elusive as the imagination, for training may stereotype the results.

Musical Example 5–1 presents a series of twenty short statements. Each has its own distinctive emotional content. No two, consecutively, are similar.

Musical Example 5–1: Green, Expressive phrases; style.

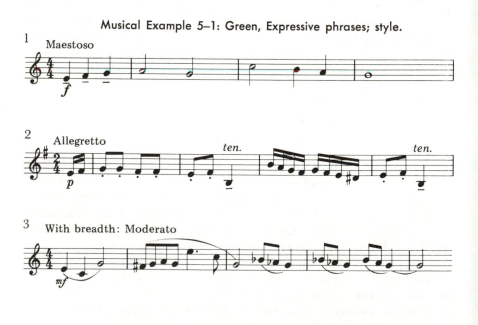

10   Moderato

11   Maestoso

12   Allegretto

13   Moderato

14   Allegro moderato

Read these excerpts through, letting the imagination roam freely. If it should happen that one or another of them brings to mind a definite picture (pictorial imagination), so much the better. As the emotional content from one to the next changes, the conductor should try to feel that change within himself. This ability to vary one's own emotional response as the music demands is also an important aspect of the conductor's art. It is one factor in making a performance come alive and negating a dead-level monotony.

MEMORY AND MEMORIZING

The two kinds of memory, "analytical" and "spontaneous," have been mentioned. Malko says, "They do not blend. The better one knows the music and the more he is accustomed to it, the more difficult it is to control the analytical line. The free-wheeling memory assumes supremacy. But as a conductor matures he may find himself concentrating too much on the conscious memory whereas, before, he relied on the subconscious. The two have to be in balance."

Most scores have dangerous places where reliance on the spontaneous memory can deceive the conductor—with unhappy results. Warning notes can be located in the preceding measures so that when these notes are heard they immediately alert the conductor to the imminent danger. Here the analytical memory functions actively in performance. In Tchaikovsky's *Romeo and Juliet Overture Fantasy* there is a difficult moment for the conductor's memory. In measure 330, the trumpets enter after 16 measures of rest. On the third beat of that same measure the cellos must be cued. Malko remarked concerning this passage, "Sometimes it is good to have words in mind . . . *after the trumpets, after the trumpets. . . ."*

To quote Malko once again: "The memory is affected by varying circumstances. If the conductor is over-tired, his memory may slip in rehearsal and performance. In this case, use the open score for the rehearsal."

Analytical Memory: Charting the Score

A conductor should be able to think through his entire score in his mind, first measure to last, without stumbling and without recourse to the score itself. Usually this process relies on the melodic lines (subconscious memory) and how they are joined together (analytical memory).

During study for memorization, the chart method may be used. In order to "chart," one must have a quick way of identifying the themes so that a kind of musical shorthand can function. The first melodic theme is usually identified by A, the second by B, and so on. Sometimes a short few measures will occur repeatedly at odd moments and here the conductor should have his own code symbol for naming them.

Chart II is a charting of Mozart's *Cosi Fan Tutte* Overture.

Chart II: Mozart, Cosi Fan Tutte Overture

Note: The designation Line 1, 2, etc., refers to the number of the lines in the chart, not to score lines. Bars are numbered to match the score.

Line 1 (Bars 1–4)

Line 2 (Bars 5–11)

co - si - fan - tut - - te - -

Line 3 (Bars 12–44) ▬ | 𝄽 || 𝄽 | 𝄽 || 𝄽 | 𝄽 ‖

Co - si - fan - tut - te

A × 4 + 2 bars | HAL! | B × 3 + 2 bars and B × 3 + 2 bars

Line 4 (Bars 45–64) A × 4 $\left(\begin{matrix} & V1 & & V1 \\ V2 & & V2 & \end{matrix}\right)$ | HAL! | D——(2 bars)

| 1st 2nd 1 bar |

Line 5 (Bars 65–95) Modulation passage 8 bars +

B × 3 + 2 bars and B × 3 + 2 bars
(Meas. 79)

Line 6 (Bars 96–114) A × 3 $\left(\begin{matrix} VI & & VI \\ & V2 & \end{matrix}\right)$ HAL! | E——(2 bars) |

| 1st 2nd 1 bar | HAL! (2 bars) |

Line 7 (Bars 115–130) A × 3 $\left(\begin{matrix} V1 & & V1 \\ & V2 & \end{matrix}\right)$ HAL! (2 bars) |

Vla.

D—— (2 bars) | | 1st 2nd 1 bar |

Line 8 (Bars 131–142) HAL! (2 bars) | A × 3 $\left(\begin{matrix} V1 & & VI \\ & V2 & \end{matrix}\right)$

HAL! (2 bars) | C—— (2 bars) |

Line 9 (Bars 143–175) | 1st 2nd 1 bar | B × 3 + 2 bars and

B × 3 + 2 bars | Modulation (8 bars + 2 bars)

Line 10 (Bars 176–209) B × 4 (fag. 4 bars; ob. 4 bars) | A × 3 $\left(\begin{matrix} V1 & & V1 \\ & V2 & \end{matrix}\right)$

HAL! (4 bars) | B × 3 + 2 bars and B × 3 + 2 bars
| Meas. 193

Line 11 (Bars 210–230) Modulation 8 bars + 2 bars | Modulation 8

bars plus

Co - si - fan -

Line 12 (Bars 231–235)   4 bars leading to

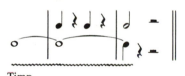

tut - - - - te

Line 13 (Bars 236–252)

Co - - si - - fan - - tut - - te (5 bars)

ending on bar 6   ⌜Winds
    A × 1 2 ⌐3 4 5 6
       C   E G C E G

Line 14 (Bars 253–261)   HAL!   (4 bars + 2 bars + 1 bar)
              C

Timp.

This overture has two themes that enter repeatedly. We have designated them as A and B. In addition, there is the constantly recurring motif: quarter note, half note, quarter note, followed by four quarter notes. It comes bursting in with its own impetuous abandon at odd moments throughout the composition. From its character, Sir Donald Tovey [1] (Reid Orchestra, Edinburgh) speaks of it as a "hallelujah." We have adopted this designation and it appears in the chart under the abbreviation of "Hal."

When the conductor can write the chart rapidly from memory while singing the themes as he writes, he can be sure that his two memory abilities are both functioning properly and that his memorizing is solid and secure.

Looking now at Chart II:

Line 1 of the chart (measures 1–4): The beginning has been clarified by rhythmic notation, the pitch sounds being carried in the mind.

Line 2 (measures 5–11): Uses the ditto marks to show the repetition of the opening bars and indicates the dangerous interlocking cue on the eighth measure.

[1] Donald Francis Tovey, *Essays in Musical Analysis,* (London: Oxford University Press, 1939), Vol. VI, p. 30.

Line 3 (measures 12–44): States the chords by solid perpendicular lines interspersed by the tutti rests. In the middle of the line we come to the double bar where the Presto begins. The first Presto theme is A. The runs in the fifteenth measure of the Presto are B. Between these two we meet the first Hal! motif: ♪ ♪ ♪ |♪ ♪ ♪ ♪ | which re-

peats itself. The A × 4 means that the A motif is repeated four times. B × 3 + 2 signifies three repetitions of the B motif plus two extra measures. Since this unit repeats itself in its entirety, it appears twice in the chart.

Line 4 (measures 45–64): The alternation of A between the second and first violins is indicated. A new marking D—— tells us that a certain set of link measures of syncopation occur on the note D. (Later in the piece they come on C.) This is followed by a five-note figure, two two-measure figures, and ending on another complete measure. The reiterations of the two-measure figure are counted out and bracketed, and the 1 at the end of the line shows the extra odd measure (the other half of the introductory five-note sequence as shown by the two-measure figure).

Line 5 (measures 65–95): Clear as indicated.

Line 6 (measures 96–114): Also clear as notated since all symbols have already been explained.

Line 7 (measures 115–130): Also clear.

Line 8 (measures 131–142): Here comes the syncopation bridge on the note C (mentioned in Line 4).

Line 9 (measures 143–175): Clear.

Line 10 (measures 176–209): Here one is reminded of the Bassoon 2 and Oboe 2 instrumentation.

Line 11 (measures 210–230): At the end of the line the chords are indicated.

Line 12 (measures 231–235): Shows the dangerous tutti rest which must be called to the conductor's attention.

Line 13 (measures 236–252): Self-explanatory. In the last of these measures the pitch of the initial note of the rhythmic figure is indicated plus the wind cue.

Line 14 (measures 253–261): Shows distinctly how the piece ends.

Having completed this long form of the chart, one studies it thoroughly, singing constantly the melody line so that the sequence of the piece hangs together in the inner ear.

When this is conquered, the chart can be abbreviated. The units are combined into larger groupings. See Chart III.

Chart III

INTRODUCTION

SECTION I   A × 5
(Bars 1–78)

                  HAL

                  B complete   lOb. Fl. Ob. Fl.
                    (C–F)

                  A × 4   VI   VI
                                V2   V2

                  HAL–4

                  Modulation 8

SECTION II   · B complete   Fag. Ob. Fag. Ob
(Bars 79–148) (G–C)

                  A × 3   Vl   Vl
                                      V2

                  HAL–4

                  HAL–2

                  A × 3   Vl   Vl
                                      V2

                  HAL–2

                  HAL–2

                  A × 3   Vl   Vl
                                      V2

                  HAL–2

Section III   B complete   Cl. Ob. Fl. Cl.   Cl. Ob. Fl. Ob.
(Bars 149–192) (F–B-flat)   Fg. Fg. Cl. Fg.

       Modulation 10

       B × 4   Fag. 2 Ob. 2
       (G–Cmin)

       A × 3   Vl   Vl
                   V2

       HAL–4

Section IV   B complete   Ob. Fl. Ob. Fl.   Same
(Bars 193–227) (C–F)   Fg.

       Modulation 8

         + 2

       Modulation 8

       Meas. 228

A   1 2 3 4 5 6   HAL
   C E G C E G   C

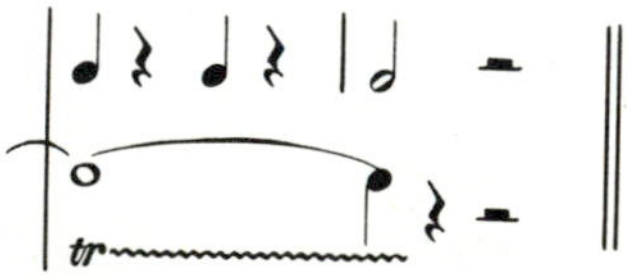

And finally, the short form emerges. Here only the broadest outlines
are shown, since the mind and ear have now mastered the complete
chart. Note how the piece divides itself into sections on the B theme,
Sections, I, II, III, IV (Chart IV).

Chart IV (Brief Form)

   INTRO
   A–HAL

I. B
   A–HAL
   MOD.

II. B
   3 sequences A–HAL    HAL

III.   B
  MOD
  B × 4   A × 3   exception
IV.   B
  MOD + 2 + MOD
  CODA

| | | ‾5‾

| | | | | | 𝄞 1 2 3 4 5 6
              C E G C E G

  HAL–C

♩ 𝄾 ♩ 𝄾 | 𝅗𝅥 ▬ ‖

Once the piece is charted, file the chart for future reference. It will save a great deal of time in reviewing repertoire months or even years later.

Spontaneous Memory

In spontaneous memory the ear memorizes many things just by hearing them repeatedly. (A child learns to talk by this means.) Melody lines are usually acquired in this way. Often an inexperienced conductor will find to his surprise that he can conduct a movement rather successfully from memory if he has heard it often enough. But total reliance on spontaneous memory is insufficient for complete security.

Eye contact with the musicians is imperative. Therefore, memorization should be completed with both kinds of memory fully activated.

Supplementary Readings *(See Appendix F)*

ADOLF F. CHRISTIANI, *Principles of Expression in Pianoforte Playing.* When applying these principles to instruments other than the piano, replace the word "accent" either with "emphasis" or "swell."

RICHARD L. CROCKER, *A History of Musical Style.*

EMIL KAHN, *Conducting,* Chapter 4, "Interpretation."

BROCK MCELHERAN, *Conducting Technique,* Chapter XX, "Thoughts on Interpretation."

NICOLAI MALKO, *The Conductor and his Baton,* pp. 210–219, "Kinetics and Agogics."

Hugo D. Marple, *The Beginning Conductor,* Chapter 20, "Style."

Leonard B. Meyer, *Emotion and Meaning in Music,* Chapter 8, "Note on Image, Processes, Connotations, and Mood," pp. 256–271.

Walter E. Nallin, *The Musical Idea.* Deals extensively with compositional forms and their development.

Carl E. Seashore, *Psychology in Music,* Chapter 14, "Imagining in Music," pp. 161–172.

Sir Donald Francis Tovey, *Essays in Musical Analysis.* All six volumes are pertinent. For *Così fan tutte,* see Volume VI, pp. 30–31.

Exercises for Practice
(Expression, Emotion, Memorization, Charting)

1. Using the material of Musical Example 5–1, play through each example and write down what it signifies to *you,* emotionally. Let your imagination go. If a picture comes into your mind (as, for example, a country dance or the flat plains of the Ukraine), make a written note of this also. Then think this picture intensely while you conduct the excerpt. Do not tell the class what you are thinking, but see if they can get some feeling for the scene (or the emotion) through your handling of the music.

2. Bring your list to class and be ready when called upon.

3. Two or three students should perform the same example. Differences in style will emerge, all good and all within the specifications

4. Obtain a recording of the *Meditation from Thaïs* by Massenet. Study it from the emotional aspect. In the opera, it is performed as an entr'acte. The heroine goes off into the desert to make a choice between her royal lover (life) and her religion (death). One finds thoughtfulness, struggle, despair, resolution, triumph, submission, and the final tranquility in this music. Use your imagination as you listen.

5. Take the Bach score, pages 150-55. Edit it fully as given on page 76. Then chart it as suggested on pages 83-85. Memorize it! See page 157 for memory suggestions as applied to this excerpt.

chapter **6**

Rehearsing the Score

Malko

There are two basic kinds of rehearsing. The first requires the same absolute perfection technically and emotionally that will transpire at the concert. The composition is "performed" in the rehearsal. A conductor of this kind may even refuse to teach the musicians by applying his own technical knowledge.

The second kind of rehearsing builds the performance gradually, both technically and artistically, even at times resorting to somewhat elementary methods, for example, taking certain passages slowly, working with separate sections and even with individual members of the ensemble. In some cases oral explanations are used. The activity here is not to perform during the rehearsal but to work systematically preparing the ultimate goal.

Editor's note: In 1964 when Sir John Barbarolli was to perform Mahler's Sixth Symphony with the Halle Orchestra in Manchester, England, he began to "teach" the music, which was new to the orchestra, by having a three-hour rehearsal in the morning with the strings, another three hours in the afternoon with the winds and percussion, and a third three-hour workout with the full orchestra in the evening. This routine went on for two days. On the third day the regular rehearsal schedule with the full orchestra was resumed.

With Nikisch one found his concerts quite different from his rehearsals. Sir Adrian Boult mentioned two cases in which Nikisch, "whipped the orchestra up emotionally for a short period of time during the rehearsal, 'just to try them out.'"

My own preference is for the second kind of rehearsing: to build, to instruct, to try out everything necessary for the future performance. I am even afraid to have the orchestra become carried away emotionally during the rehearsal. Please do not misunderstand! Being carried away emotionally and being completely absorbed in the work at hand are two different things. Especially do I fear having the conductor carried away with the music itself. In such cases he may forget his duties as the master of the rehearsal and may begin, instead, to soar into the clouds.

In conducting a semi-professional orchestra, one must hear what is actually sounding and not become entranced with the music instead. In rehearsal one cannot afford to deceive oneself.

In addressing his orchestra Hans Richter made the following remark: "First of all, the pleasure of making music for you and myself, and then we will think of the audience." Upon one occasion a member of his orchestra (not a professional conductor) conducted a performance at Grinzing near Vienna. The next day he said to Richter, "You know, it is not difficult at all to conduct!" With a confidential smile Richter replied, *"Pst . . . verraten Sie uns nicht!"* (Don't give us away!) Naturally this kind of heartwarming charm has a universal appeal.

There is also the true story about a player who went to his conductor and said, "You know your stuff well. But I have a request to make. Please don't look at me. It makes me nervous."

Bruno Walter made it a rule not to cue a nervous player provided he knew the player was competent and thoroughly acquainted with his part. Mr. Walter would look away instead.

A real master-conductor knows his instrument thoroughly and understands how best to bring forth great music from it.

At one professional orchestra rehearsal under a well-known conductor the following incident took place: At the first rehearsal questions had been asked by the piccolo player and the trombonist. The same thing happened at the second rehearsal and this time there were a few listeners in the auditorium. Suddenly a "performance" started. The conductor threw himself into a veritable tantrum.

Another time, with a different orchestra and a different conductor, a similar incident took place. The poor musician who had asked the question ran from the stage more dead than alive in order to escape the conductor's wrath.

Such happenings are a disgrace to the profession. The rehearsal is the place where questions should be asked when necessary and the conductor should help the musicians in every way possible toward the goal of the finest future performance. A conductor has no right to substitute a blind rage and a threatening fist for a professionally thoughtful attitude toward human beings.

But things are not always thus. One remembers the story of the bassoonist who became incensed beyond control, sprang from his chair, and started for the conductor brandishing his instrument. In self-preservation the conductor jumped off the stand and ran for the exit, the flailing bassoonist in hot pursuit. (It is a true story.)

TIMING THE REHEARSAL

The tempo of rehearsals is different with different orchestras and different conductors. Sometimes a conductor rehearses for two hours on one piece and then gallops through the rest of the program during the remaining half hour. This rarely insures a completely satisfactory concert.

The conductor should know, and plan, how to allot to each composition the necessary division of his rehearsal time. He should not agree to just one or two rehearsals unless he knows how to use the time efficiently and effectively and can thereafter appear before the audience with a clear conscience.

Sometimes a conductor is fortunate enough to have sufficient time to play completely through everything on the program, stopping at the necessary spots for intensive rehearsing. But this is not always the case. Therefore, in his initial planning, he must carefully consider the time factor.

PLANNING THE REHEARSAL

The rehearsal should be systematically planned ahead of time. As the conductor studies his scores he must be alert to notice the things that may cause trouble or be difficult for the players: dynamic balance, difficult rhythms, dangerous entrances, and so on. He should prepare his solutions and his means for handling these places during his study time. But he should not decide beforehand, "Here I shall stop them and tell them. . . ." The conductor should be ready with his solutions in case they are needed, but he should not stop when the orchestra is already efficient in those places.

The conductor should also have ready in mind what sections of the compositions can "carry themselves," where he can safely skip pages in the rehearsal if time should run short.

If he is well prepared, the wise conductor has also rehearsed his own technique. He has practiced on his "mute keyboard." He has rehearsed his gestures. This statement may cause some conductors to smile, but a conductor's gestures are his technique, and checking them in front of a mirror to *test their clarity* is not so strange.

Furtwangler once said, almost in surprise, *"Le Sacre du Printemps* —it is so difficult I had to practice it!" (Say this to a violinist or a pianist!)

What is the conductor's ultimate goal in designing his rehearsal? Obviously, to build a musical structure that will solidly stand its test in front of the audience.

Finesse of style, the musical sense of the composition, the correct appraisal of its emotional drive, an alive pulsation, a warm heart: to show all of this to the orchestra, talent alone is not enough. It is not sufficient to have a highly developed musical background. It is not enough to have a serious and deep knowledge of music in general and of the particular score in question. Something more is needed.

Let us compare the conductor to the builder of buildings. The builder may know well how to read his blueprint, but he must also know how to build the edifice. He must know how to place the bricks, how to fasten them, where to put the nails, where to place the beams supporting the ceiling, and which material to select for each section of the building. In short, he must know not only how a structure is laid out in the preliminary plan, but also how finally to put it together.

A conductor likewise must know how to construct his edifice. He should live his rehearsal in his imagination. He should plan a logical sequence in his presentation of the problems in the music to be performed. He, too, has to lay his bricks consistently, choose his supporting beams, and decide on the texture of his materials.

In his preliminary planning the conductor has to recognize where the melody is paramount and controls the flow of the music and where, contrariwise, the rhythmic drive forces the melody to submit. He has balanced his forces in his imagination. He has inaudibly "heard" the various tone qualities and textures of the instruments of the orchestra and decided on the kind of sound he wishes to have brought forth here and there in the score. Only when his imagination of the music has matured and become an all-controlling force is he ready to stand in front of the musicians and become their leader. His aim is to bring their audible rendition into line with the ideal heights already heard by his inner ear.

When the conductor is finally fully prepared, he presents himself before the orchestra ready to rehearse.

CONDUCTING THE REHEARSAL

Since the conductor presents himself fully prepared, the rehearsal then becomes one for the benefit of the players—and the composer.

The conductor should, first of all, create and maintain rhythmic order among his performers. His first words after "Good morning, gentlemen," and the title of the composition to be rehearsed are "In two" or "In four" or whatever his time-beating pattern is to be. This is basic to mutual understanding.

The movements of the conductor's hands and arms serve as signals for the musicians. These movements are the conductor's tools with which to construct his building. It is very difficult to create a beautiful structure if the tools are faulty and dull.

Having established rhythmic order, the conductor must next solve the problem of how to bridge the gap from time-beating to his individual interpretation. This implies that his motions must be in character and accord with his musical ideas. These motions must be able to describe the music itself, not just to beat it.

He must rehearse the difficult spots, understanding why they are difficult and what to do about it. He may find it necessary upon occasion to call separate rehearsals (sectionals) for the strings or the winds or percussion. At times he may resort to a slow tempo followed thereafter by the required tempo, reinserting the passage into the composition.

And throughout all of this he consciously or subconsciously keeps a finger on the pulse of his musicians, judging their reactions to what is transpiring. He senses the depth of their involvement in the music itself and their degree of willingness to cooperate in working toward a fine musical effect.

Different conductors work in different ways. With Mahler, at a certain moment of great intensity, the movements of his arm were seen gradually to diminish, reaching the absolute minimum, not using the baton but resorting momentarily only to the fingertips, his eyes alone remaining active. This kind of intensity was the result of training and a true technical mastery.

As conductors we must never forget that a technical means always corresponds to the artistic demands of the music. Nothing exterior should affect the movement. Volume and character of time beating should not upset the rhythm. As was said before, music is in constant motion, changes coming measure by measure. As the conductor leads these changes with his motions, the basic inner drive of the forward motion should not be upset.

Regarding the mechanics of stopping the orchestra in the rehearsal: Too many stops immediately on the heels of each other are psychologically unsound and cause frustration and nervousness. For example, the beginning of the Tchaikovsky Sixth Symphony:

Stop————intonation
Stop————ensemble
Stop————double piano
Stop————take it up-bow

It is far better to play the phrase, make one stop, and then request several corrections at one time.

Editor's note: A tragic example of this was seen at the second Nicolai Malko International Competition for Young Conductors in Copenhagen in 1968. One young man was so anxious to prove that he was hearing everything that he stopped the orchestra almost every measure. The line of the music had no chance to establish itself as such before he stopped again. After some twenty minutes of this foolishness the musicians and the judges were completely frustrated, as well as the young man himself. Nothing of a musical character had transpired. The young man was eliminated on the first round—he had eliminated himself!

It is not advisable to go through a whole movement, talking it off, before playing. This is generally a waste of time because certain things may already have been accomplished by the musicians without the preliminary "lecture." It is better to begin to play and then make the corrections when and where they are needed.

BEYOND THE GESTURE: TALKING

Members of a professional orchestra, chorus, or band depend on the conductor to varying degrees. They are, in a sense, subordinate to him (and dependent on him) not only as participating musicians but also from the standpoint of earning their living. Since this is true, it is possible that in speaking one may be tempted also to command.

Obviously, there are certain things that can be expressed in words that would be impossible to show by gesture alone, but because this is true, the temptation is great to express one's intentions *only* by words. The more one is able to show the less he will find it necessary to talk. When he does talk, it should be brief and to the point.

It is impossible, of course, never to speak during the rehearsal. Sometimes a technical admonition in words is very useful. There are also occasions when a simile or descriptive word suddenly creates a bridge to the desired musical understanding—the phrase, the dynamic, a certain nuance or tone color.

Editor's note: This brings to mind Victor Kolar's[1] request to the first violin section: "A tone like sunlight on polished brass" and Malko's notation on the Leonore No. 3, "as if the sun came out."

In Tchaikovsky's *Romeo and Juliet* overture-fantasy, after the love

---

[1] Victor Kolar was conductor of the Detroit Symphony and later of the Detroit's Women's Symphony Orchestra. Dates are not available.

theme, there is a passage of tender, rustling sounds in the violins. Nikisch said, "Like a whisper of lovers under the lilac tree." And again in the coda to the Pathetique (first movement), the pizzicato in the strings, "Like drops of spring rain."

The story of Toscanini's tossing his handkerchief into the air and letting it float "comme ça" is famous. It happened during his rehearsal in Paris of *Le Festin d'Arregnier* by Albert Roussel. His demonstration indeed corresponded to the light, floating character of the musical moment in question.

Such associative indications may be at times very useful but only if they produce a positive result in the ensuing musical sound. If not, they are useless. And often a word of technical advice—what to do on the instrument itself or with the bow—will produce more immediately the desired effect, especially if it is spoken not rudely but respectfully and to the point.

I have myself often asked the chorus members to smile. This resulted in the necessary coloring of the sound.

A classic anecdote is Sir Thomas Beecham's speech to the ladies of the chorus who were singing "For unto us a child is born." "Ladies, the composer wanted it to sound artistic, not realistic. Try to present not the pain of childbearing but the joy of child birth." Such humor in limited measure and without excessiveness can be useful.

One cannot help regretting the fact that too often the members of the chorus or orchestra hear rude remarks that cut deeply and are at times even uncivil. The light touch is more gratefully received.

In Vienna, Hans Richter reprimanded a double-bass player. The man answered, "You are right. I made a mistake. But why so nasty? Maestro, if you had a little bell at the end of your baton we might hear some wrong notes too—sometimes."

CONDUCTORIAL BEHAVIOR IN REHEARSAL

The behavior of conductors in rehearsal is a special topic. It is closely connected to the problems of the social order. In most cases bad behavior on the conductor's part is the result of his acceptance of his power. Is it not also true that his bad behavior is caused by a lack of understanding of the true substance of conducting?

When Toscanini used to lose his temper, it was taken in stride by his musicians. He would start shouting abuse in four languages simultaneously which few, if any, understood. In Paris and Vienna the players simply ignored it. Once in Vienna he had a real tantrum. He threw the music on the floor and started stamping on it. Since he did not see very well, he trampled the floor *next to the music*—either by chance or by design. The first violinist pointed with his bow and said quietly, "It's over here, Maestro."

Toscanini has become a legend in his own right. It is difficult to find in any domain such legendary popularity, but this in no way detracts from his musical significance as one of the greatest of conductors, possessing truly exceptional conducting talents.

We have mentioned the talkative conductor. Wilhelm Mengelberg is the classic example of this kind of conductor in rehearsal. His musical fame rests on the magnificent training he gave to the Concertgebow Orchestra of the Netherlands. His effect on that orchestra is still felt. In Holland he was treated as a deity.

In Russian there is a proverb that says, "Whoever takes a stick is a corporal." This proverb is very well suited to those who become conductors. Mengelberg is no exception. He was, first of all, a boss, a dictator, and a *prima donna*. He had all of the inherent qualities. He was also an egotist and very vain, but nevertheless a genuinely professional conductor.

But Mengelberg liked to talk. He talked in the rehearsal without stopping. A violinist from the Concertgebow told of rehearsing the *Fantastic Symphony* of Berlioz. This work starts out very slowly, Adagio. The violins enter on the third bar. They sat, almost the whole rehearsal with bows lifted, ready to come in—and never played a single note. Mengelberg had been speaking all the time about the first two bars.

By the end of the last rehearsal before a concert, Mengelberg would suddenly realize that he had rehearsed only one composition and had not touched the others. Then he would rush through the rest of the program, sometimes not even looking at some of the works. Still, since he was an excellent conductor, things would not go badly at the concert.

It is now proper to remark that in conducting, as in other things, people are prone to imitate first the obvious features that easily attract attention. The subtler and more worthy aspects of genius are ignored. It is far easier to imitate the obvious.

One finds it difficult to imagine how many conductors have tried to imitate Toscanini's behavior and lack of restraint rather than his superb musicianship. And what a quantity of chatterers have been bred by Mengelberg's talkativeness! It is hard to appraise such garrulousness, but I am sure it is not so very useful after all.

One last anecdote as a warning to young conductors: It happened in Budapest. A conductor became riled, "I will leave. I won't conduct." His agent took out his watch and said, "If you hurry, you can catch the five o'clock train." As you may have guessed the conductor did not depart.

Another time this same conductor was rude to the orchestra. They simply refused to play until he apologized. He fumed and raged, but finally he gave in.

FOR WHOM DO YOU PERFORM?

All of the training, all of the score study, all of the rehearsing have as their ultimate goal the presentation before an audience.

When the conductor thoroughly knows what he is doing, it is possible for the audience to listen with ears *and eyes,* and with every facet of the faculties one uses to appreciate an artistic performance—yes, including one's own imagination.

There are singers who have less than first-class voices, but who are so convincing and exciting in their presentations that they produce results denied others who may be equipped with better natural voices but who lack the necessary "know-how."

Once in a private home Artur Schnabel asked me, "For whom do you perform?"

"For the listener," I answered.

"For the audience?" Schnabel was appalled.

"But for whom do you perform?" I then asked.

Schnabel lifted his arms, rolled his eyes heavenward and said, with the voice of a high priest, "For the music."

Be our performance philosophy what it may, it in no way diminishes our own admiration for and dedication to this great art or our continual striving for the highest ideal. The better the performance, the more joy it will bring to the audience and to the performing musicians. This should never be forgotten.

The composer, the performer, the listener, these three form one united, organic phenomenon. In its completed circle it is the essence of musical art.

Supplementary Readings *(See Appendix F)*

Adrian C. Boult, *A Handbook on the Technique of Conducting,* Section VIII, "Rehearsal."

Benjamin Grosbayne, *Techniques of Modern Orchestral Conducting,* Chapters 21–24.

Charles Munch, *I Am a Conductor,* Chapter VI, "Rehearsing."

Exercises for Practice

1. Take either the Bach or Mahler excerpt, pages 141 and 150 and build a rehearsal plan. State the number of players in each section of your imaginary ensemble. Give their probable degree of technical advancement. Consider dynamic balance among the parts as you make your rehearsal plan. Your time will be one hour. If you prefer, choose a band score, edit it, and build the rehearsal plan for the first eight pages of the score.
2. Organize a small wind ensemble and conduct it in pertinent repertoire. Edit your score, phrasing, dynamics, cues.
3. Obtain the four-hand piano scores of the Haydn and Beethoven symphonies. Find pianists who will play them for you as you conduct. (Students in the Conservatory in Moscow are assigned certain hours each week conducting two-piano teams.)
4. As a last resort, get an orchestra or band recording and conduct it. Show your dynamics, think balance, throw your cues in the right direction. Try to get involved with the emotional aspect of the music. Drive, don't follow, when working with the recordings. Use your ear in a discriminatory way.

chapter 7

Comments on and Evaluations

of Specific Composers

Malko

Editor's note: As the reader has progressed through this book he may have already surmised (and correctly so) that Nicolai Malko was personally acquainted with most of the world-renowned musicians of our time. He conducted all of Chaliapin's roles with that great basso in the lead. He conducted for Pavlova, Nijinsky, Karsavina, Fokine, and Legat. His soloists included Prokofieff, Stravinsky, Hindemith, Stern, Piatigorsky, Horowitz, Brailowsky, Levine, Oistrakh, Heifetz, Fournier, Firkusny, Bachauer, Christoff, Schwartzkopf, Pierce, Price, Merrill, Ferrell, Francescatti, and a host of others. Malko and Stravinsky often occupied a booth at the Bronnum restaurant in Copenhagen after their performance. Malko had a brilliant and trained mind that worked with the speed of lightning. He was also fairminded. His comments and evaluations carry the weight of authority and are valuable to the conductors of the future. The following excerpts come from his notes for this book and from correspondence still extant.

STRAVINSKY

Stravinsky enjoys looking over his works and publishing new editions. His orchestration of the *Firebird Suite* for a small orchestra (1919) is extremely good and undoubtedly sounds better than the original version made for an augmented orchestra. This I discovered for myself, having conducted the whole ballet in the first version, and the Suite in both the first and second versions.

Once I conducted this Suite in Chicago and suddenly I heard something new coming from the orchestra. I asked Stravinsky, "Why staccato in the last 7/4" (Doppio valore, Figure 19)?

"Oh, this is a new version. I want it staccato." This made me sad. In the score it read *Maestoso,* and it is so agreeable to hear these chords *tenuto, pesante* as a contrast to the previous staccato of the quick tempo.

As is known, *Petrushka* was written for an augmented orchestra. Later a new version for the customary instrumentation appeared. I definitely prefer the first, original version.

In *Oedipus Rex,* in the new version, some of the bar groups are changed (the bar divisions). At times this seems to be of no consequence because the coexistence of simultaneous themes of different rhythmic values never will settle into bars of homogeneous rhythm. Composers find it very possible to write simultaneously in different rhythms using separate lines in the score, for example, *A Life for the Czar* by Glinka, third act, Hindemith's *Weber Variations,* and so on. In practice, it does not help the conducting because it becomes necessary to conduct in one rhythm with the baton while only the virtuoso left hand of the conductor can help with the second rhythm.

The final dance of *Le Sacre du Printemps* was reworked several times because of these cross rhythms. The bar-lines created a problem both for the composer and the conductor. Koussevitsky found them difficult. Much later a separate edition of this Dance appeared (the renowned Figure 142 in the music). Stravinsky assured me that in this edition everything was simple and would go by itself. With great difficulty I arranged to give a performance of this newer writing in Copenhagen. (They had to pay a double performance fee—one for the ballet publisher and another for the new version of the Dance itself.) However, I cannot say that this new version made it any easier for the orchestra or the conductor since by that time everyone was accustomed to the "usual" version. Of course, this spot is very difficult, but after detailed work everything settles into the right place and comes out very well. I was convinced of this recently in Tokyo with an orchestra that had never played *Le Sacre* before.

Simplifications do not always help. Once Ziloti decided to change Dukas' *Sorcerer's Apprentice.* He made one bar out of three bars—one bar of 3/4 from three bars of 3/8. The poor musicians did not know what to do. All of their attention was centered on the quarter and eighth rests. (In the French editions it is difficult to distinguish the quarter rest from the eighth rest.) Now there were many added rests written in by hand. It became impossible.

The Stravinsky *Divertissement* is a remarkably fine piece, and it is possible to play it beautifully and in a refined manner (which is how it should be played). It is very effective. Only at the end is one surprised for, as usual with Stravinsky, it does not build up. Also in the Adagio the transitions are not always convincing.

I did not know—or rather, meet with—Stravinsky during his twelve-tone period.

PROKOFIEFF

Speaking of *Les Portraits*—this work is certainly kaleidoscopic. It is positively painful to learn it by heart.

Editor's note: A bit of a feud: Prokofieff wrote to Malko to ask his "frank opinion" of Les Portraits. *Malko, too honestly, wrote back that it did not "hang together" properly—the "seams showed." Prokofieff, who was both impulsive and at times irritable, wrote back, "You conductors never take time to study our scores properly." Malko then proceeded to memorize the score from cover to cover to prove that his opinion was valid and authoritative.*

Malko continues: In memorizing this composition *(Les Portraits)* one's memory is continuously disrupted, both at the rehearsals and at the performances. The reason has to do with the bridge passages where it can move either this way or that. The "stitches" show in the "seams" and it is this lack of true symphonism and logic in Prokofieff's music that makes it difficult.

In the *Romeo Suite:* The music is attractive, especially in the rhythms, but as soon as there is need for development, the music jerks on the same spot, piling up but not progressing.

Editor's note: Regarding a Copenhagen performance of a Prokofieff composition, Malko writes: "Gay and sharp—poignant—this is the only way to save this music which is helpless in the symphonic sense. It lacks logic."

MIASKOVSKY

Symphony No. 13: Miaskovsky composes the odd-numbered works for himself. This music was under the influence of Stravinsky, both at the beginning and at the end—too bad! The harmony is sticky and difficult; the Scherzo has complicated and difficult rhythms, but it still preserves a certain formalism. There is much that is good and the music is spirited. However, there are also some indifferent spots. It was difficult for the audience and thankless for the listener. They did not like it.

KABELEVSKY

In his Second Symphony one finds traces of Korsakoff, Tchaikovsky, and others. His strongest facet is his temperament and cultural technique.

GLINKA

What a wonder Glinka's orchestra is!

SCRIABIN

Third Symphony: The audience got tired, especially in the first movement. Cuts were suggested. I objected at first, but then I agreed. On the 6/8, make a short cadence—perhaps this would be a possibility. However, each instance of cutting must be carefully considered, otherwise fine music is lost. This would be a pity.

TCHAIKOVSKY

Pique Dame—the *Song of the Card Players:* It is dangerous not to start the quick tempo immediately, for once the slower tempo is set the orchestra does not give in.

J. STRAUSS

Die Fliedermaus: Small works sometimes produce less response than one might expect, for example, *Die Fliedermaus.* It was suggested after the performance that the last bar was not loud enough, that it seemed to be building immensely toward a climax and suddenly it leveled off. Of course, I am the reason. Besides it is difficult to play ♫♩ ff—it is too quick to sound. This remark is extremely useful. I remember the last chord in the Miaskovsky Fifth. It was the same in Kharkov—the last chord was weaker than the one preceding it.

LETTERS

On March 3, 1931, Malko wrote: I felt some threshold being crossed in the development of my conducting, in the sense of preserving self-control while abandoning myself to making music.

Then on January 31, 1938: The qualities of the Halle Orchestra (Manchester, England) and their feeling for me creates something most precious—the elemental upheaval in the music itself. It happened with the *Tannhauser*, some in the de Falla, and especially in Tchaikovsky's Fifth Symphony.

From a letter to Sherman, March 3, 1959: One should not consider sentiment as something superficial. It depends on the point of view. For example, today I had two orchestra rehearsals and one for the chorus. At the first rehearsal the French baritone Souzay sang the *Salve Regina* by Monteverdi in an extremely sentimental way and it turned out very convincingly. Then he did a bass aria from Haydn's *The Seasons*—joyfully, nothing more. But when he started the *Evening Star* from *Tannhauser*, I, as conductor, was almost flabbergasted. It was the embodiment of German Romanticism in the purest, most beautiful sense of the word. Finally he sang Mephisto from Berlioz' *Faust*. He did it with an infectious gaiety but it was, I think, Berlioz' salon style virtuous Mephisto. Even Gounod's Mephisto has more of the devil (theatrical, of course) in it.

From a letter to Miaskovsky, March 10, 1932 (discussing the original version of *Boris Godounov*): It is necessary to perform (to perform, not to examine and study) the original version of the composer. It is easy to prove its vitality, its right to live on. Everybody remembers the version of Rimsky-Korsakoff. Everybody seems to feel that not everything in the composer's original version is practical, but that certain things have to be overcome in order to gain something. Everyone asks me, "Which is better?" and I am tired of replying that it is impossible to put the question in this form. (The original is a different work and requires some editing to push out the false places; some rewriting has to be done.)

I completely agree with Igor Glebov, who said in one of his books that it is perfectly possible to perform the first edition of Moussorgsky and that it is viable and theatrical.

However, to perform this work without some editing is a bit non-sensical. It is axiomatic that such a procedure belongs to the field of archeology and is not predicated on an alive approach. People who are carried away by the idea of stressing the original writing forget that *Boris* will be seen and listened to by millions of people of different countries and different nationalities who are not in the least concerned with research on Moussorgsky. They want only an alive theatrical performance.

I recollect that Meyerhold (the famous stage director) dug out a pile of preliminary notes for *The Inspector General* which had been discarded by Gogol himself, and Meyerhold asserted that his (Meyerhold's) version was the genuine one. I would also remark that in the case of Moussorgsky his editors were undoubtedly carried away when they declared Moussorgsky was hostile to any cuts in his operas. For me, Moussorgsky is such an alive and theatrical composer that I do not believe he would object to cuts that genuinely enhance the performance. Perhaps some cuts were suggested that were contrary to his theatrical sense and therefore did not improve the performance. But I also believe that certain cuts were made with his acquiescence and conviction—as the piano score of 1874.

EDITOR'S SUMMATION

Great music has a right to great effort. A casual philosophy does not bespeak honesty on the part of the conductor. To understand completely with the mind, to train the hands for musical clarity and precision of statement, to cultivate the imagination, to acquire a professional self-control, to be "alive," and to respect the composer—these are the textures of the Malko conducting philosophy. Coupled with a passion for making beautiful music they constitute art-in-time in its purest and highest form.

chapter **8**

The Contemporary Score

Green

In order to come into realistic focus in the second half of the twentieth century, a book on *The Conductor and His Score* must include the phenomena of the contemporary score.

A conductor, in studying the works of composers such as Boulez, Berio, Cage, Gerhard, Kagel, Karkoschka, Lutolawski, Messiaen, Penderecki, Stockhausen, and many others, will find a myriad of new ideas, new sounds, new symbols with which to deal. He will see that music no longer tramps across the page in horizontal lines. Instead, it may proceed in any direction of the compass; in squares, in circles, in sinuous lines that cross and interlace, in black-and-white geometric motifs that resemble contemporary abstract art, even encompassing a pictorial beauty that echoes Mondrian, Klee, Pollock, and Kandinsky.

HISTORICAL BACKGROUND

The foundations for what is happening now were laid by Schoenberg and his disciples, who added a new conception of the harmonic language, and by Stravinsky, whose genius in the exploration of intricate rhythms further expanded the horizon for composers of music. Webern's fragmented themes combined with rhythmic variations demanded new skeletons for their support and so the traditional musical forms were superseded by new forms and structures.

Throughout these earlier years of change the composers continued to use the traditional symbols for pitch notation and rhythmic indications. The complications, while great for the conductor, were instantly recognizable as such. His problem became one of "how to beat it" and how to make it as easy as possible for the players to function with a good semblance of reliability.

Time-beating pattern variations in the fives and sevens were designed to depict accurately the *inner structure of the measure*. The nineteenth-century three-beats-plus-two-beats (and vice versa) for the measure in five gave way to the modern "deleted six" pattern, thus confirming the unity of the bar rather than its division. Irregular or "lop-sided" time-beating appeared, the regularity of the takt being interrupted by the addition of an extra half beat here and there.

Cross rhythms and cross time signatures, plus the concomitant difficulty with patterns and cues, enlarged the technical demands for the conductor.

And now, once again, the contemporary score plunges ahead, going a step beyond the composer himself to explore the imagination of the performer, be he conductor or player. The composer sets the stage, so to speak, establishes the "situation," points the direction, and then watches with interest to see what ideas the performers may contribute to the working out of the plot.

CONTEMPORARY MORES

New sounds (often non-musical in character) begin to appear in the concert hall. The emphasis turns toward tone color, texture, and sound effect. Melodic use of pitch and steadiness of rhythm become secondary facets, often disappearing completely from the composition.

The glissando, the use of high-pitched harmonic sounds, percussive techniques applied to all instruments (sometimes to the physical detriment of the instrument itself) are being diligently explored. Electronic sounds and computerized renderings are used to enhance still further the resultant sound effects.

The reader may be referred to the recording of Krzysztof Penderecki's *Threnody to the Victims of Hiroshima*.[1] Written for fifty-two stringed instruments and *no other sources of sound*, the work is phenomenal in its emotional effectiveness and in the almost unbelievable sounds coming from this galaxy of strings. Such a work has already become part of the "permanent repertoire," at least in its recorded form.

---

[1] Recorded by Polskie Nagrania Warszawa Muza BIEM XL0171a, Poland. Also by Victor Records, VICS 1239 (recorded in Italy); and by Philips, PHS 2901 (also Warsaw).

THE CONDUCTOR AND HIS CONTEMPORARY SCORE

In many scores, the conductor is free to make his beat (his "signal") when he deems best. Some composers state definitely the number of seconds to elapse between signals. Others show varying distances on the page between the signals (the "bar-lines"), thus leaving the timing to the discretion of the conductor.

Although certain effects are indicated by the composer, the actual pitches are often left unstated. The general contour of the melodic line may be shown, but not its sounding notes. Conductor and players choose and decide what shall realistically transpire. Pertinent choices may concern pitch, rhythm, duration, timing, and so on. Cues for new entrances may be freely given as the conductor molds the sound *after* having heard and judged its texture, dynamics, and other audible factors.

Thus exactitude has given way to an emancipated flexibility and we find ourselves confronted with the age of unpredictable "happenings."

And since happenings are neither predictable nor controllable, new signs and symbols—a new notation—had to be invented to handle the performance freedoms. Here is where the composer's individualism has achieved its oneness. Because of the vast panorama now opening before the composer, each man has explored his own imagination, gone in his own direction, and invented his own symbols with which to state his boundaries for the freedom he will allow. This kind of notation is termed "spaced notation."

Composers customarily include in the score a table of definitions for the signs used. It is the conductor's job to assimilate these symbols and teach them to the players. He then guides and supervises the performance, showing by his signals when each happening is to start, cueing entrances and showing cut-offs, and balancing the sounds against each other.

KARKOSCHKA'S RESEARCH

The great treatise on modern notation, *Das Schriftbild der neuen Musik* by Erhard Karkoschka,[2] is in German. Karkoschka has systematically examined the work of our twentieth-century composers and has

---

[2] Edition Moeck, No. 4010, Celle (Germany), Hermann Moeck Verlag, copyright 1966.

An English translation of this work is also available: *Notation in New Music, A Critical Guide to Interpretation and Realization,* trans. Ruth Koenig (New York: Frederick A. Praeger, Inc., 1972).

listed their many *individual approaches to notation,* carefully classified as to pitch, timing, instrumentation, instrumental techniques, duration of sound, and so on. It is a magnificent work. Every conceivable kind of score appears therein. The reader will find some scores using the standard symbols; other scores show none of the traditional notation. Electronic music is also covered, together with the electronic score and the reduced score.

Stockhausen's *Refrain for Three Players,* as quoted in Karkoschka (pp. 156–157), shows a series of score-lines in a kind of circular formation with a transparent rotating band superimposed.

Two of the most interesting, pictorially, of the scores quoted in Karkoschka are shown here in Musical Examples 8–1 and 8–2. The *Cycloide I, II, III* and *I + II + III* by Logothetis have great graphic charm. (See pages 111 and 112.)

The first page of the *Cycloide* is comprised of twelve interlocking lines, straight and curved, intermingled and whirling, representing twelve voices or parts. The second page is a galaxy of expanding stars and accents, and page three reminds one of a line drawing by Virgil Partch. Superimposing the three pages upon each other, a conglomerate is formed with a gray-tone color added.

Differing in appearance, but no less visually interesting, is the charming design depicted in Moran's *Four Visions, No. 2* (Musical Example 8–2, page 113).

The instrumentation of the *Four Visions, No. 2* is given as flute, harp, and string quartet. The time of performance is between one minute fifteen seconds and one minute thirty-five seconds.

GRASPING THE SCORE COMPLEXITIES

The easiest and most logical introduction to the complexities of modern writing is through the examination of the publications now available for instructional purposes and school use. The score forms, although contemporary, are simplified and quickly understood. Complete tables of symbols are given in each composition.

Many such scores come from the Verlag Universal Edition (London and Vienna) and are obtainable in the United States from Theodore Presser Company, Bryn Mawr, Pennsylvania.

Musical Example 8–3 shows a rather "standard" kind of blocked-out score format (page 113).

Musical Example 8–1: Logothetis, Cycloide I, II, III, and I + II + III.

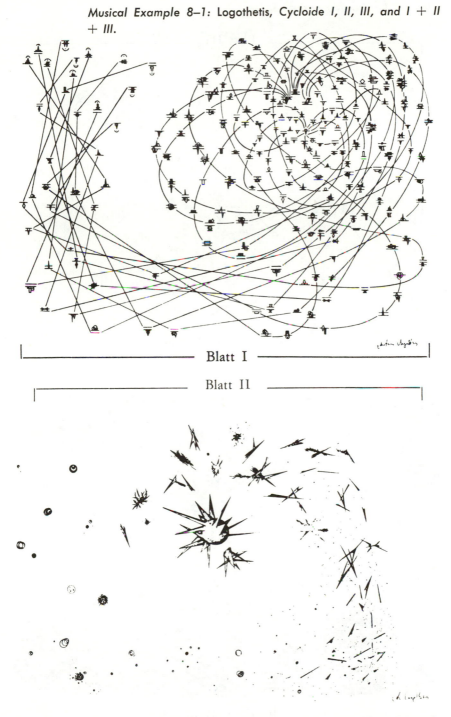

Blatt I

Blatt II

Reprinted by permission of Edition Modern, Musikverlag Hans Wewerka, Munich.

Blatt III

Blatt I + II + III

Musical Example 8–2: Moron, *Four Visions*, No. 2.

© 1964 Universal Edition A. G., Vienna. Used by permission of the publisher. Theodore Presser Company sole representative United States, Canada and Mexico.

Musical Example 8–3: The "charted score."

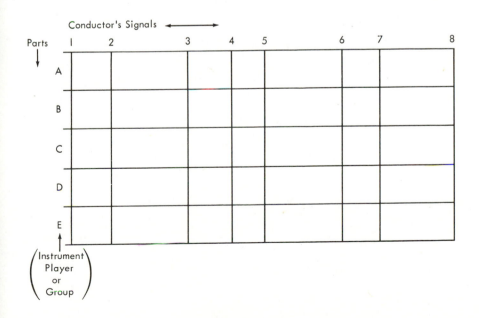

Note that the number of parts is listed by letters in the left-hand margin. The perpendicular lines dividing the page into rectangles signify beats or "signals" to be made by the conductor. The position of the notational symbol, high or low, within each rectangle gives a clue as to the tessitura of the pitch to be sounded. Choice of pitch is left to the player, unless otherwise specified.

In his *Contemporary Primer for Band,* Sydney Hodkinson uses a score-form as shown in Musical Example 8–4.

Within each major rectangle there runs a median line designating the median range for instruments of that family. The placement of the symbol above or below the median line indicates (by its distance from the line) the range of the instrument and height of the pitch to be sounded. Again, the choice of actual pitch is left to the players.

Sometimes a standard two- or four-beat pattern is requested from the conductor. Some composers suggest that the signals be given always with the same hand, the other hand indicating the cues and dynamics. *Staccato* and *tenuto* gestures are hinted at.

When dots appear in the score, the spacing and density of dots indicates the speed of reiteration. The size of the symbol often refers to dynamic—the larger, the louder. The *forte-piano* (f/p) symbol requests an alternation of *forte* and *piano* on the notes executed.

Table 8–1, will clarify other meanings for the reader.

Musical Example 8–4: Sydney Hodkinson, Contemporary Primer for Band, score set-up.

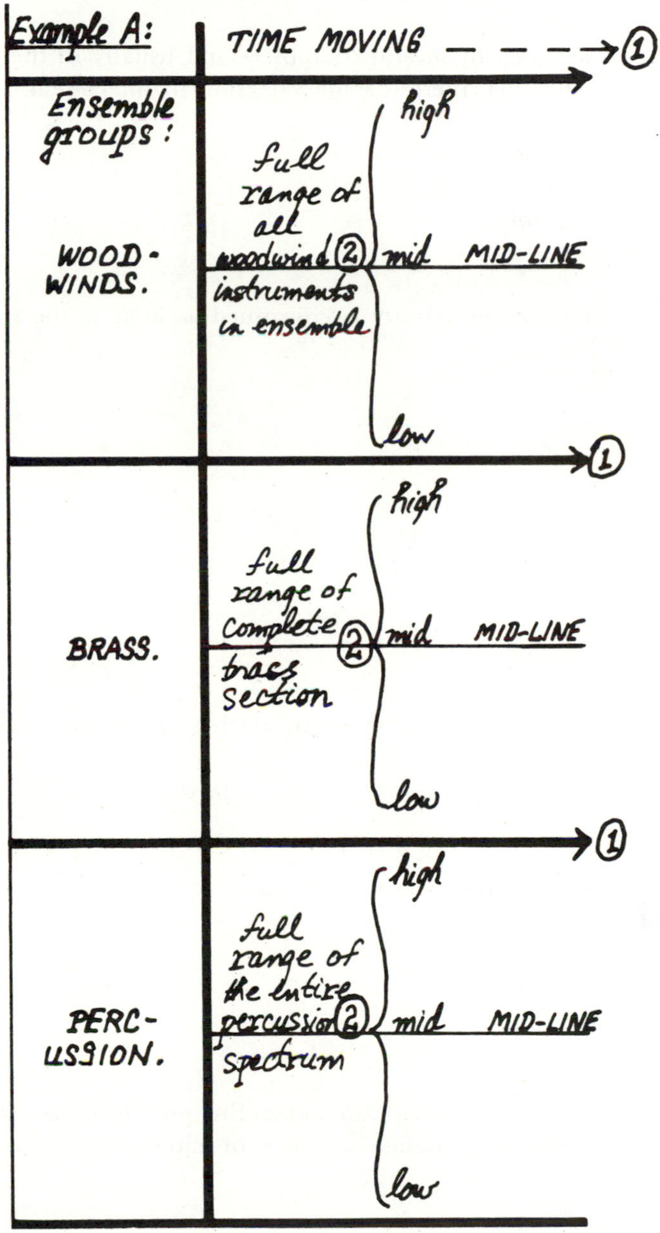

Table 8–1: Somewhat Standardized Symbols

These symbols are used by several composers and usually in the manner indicated here. However, there is some variation in interpretation.

1. ●   A short note.

2. ○   A long note.

3.   The note or activity is continued as long as the line lasts.

> or
>
> ▭
>
> or
>
> ▬

4. ▷   Reading from left to right, getting gradually softer.

5. ◁   Reading from left to right, getting gradually louder.

6. ■ or ⊔   A tone cluster.

7. 〰〰   Tremolo or vibrato, depending on the composer. Width of scallops designates speed of reiterations: the narrower, the faster.

> or ○̿
>
> or ∿∿∿∿∿

8. Glissando: indicates also direction of glissando.

or

or

9. 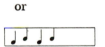 Glissando from a small range to a large range to a small range.

10. Crescendo-diminuendo.

11. Alternate the notes as long as the line or rectangle lasts.

or

12. f/p Alternate loud and soft.

13. Let the tone ring, dying away at its own speed.

14. Shows pitch contour.

15. Sound is to be repeated.

or . . . . . .

16. Sound repeated, getting faster

17. Sound repeated, getting slower.

18. Arrows are used to show direction of rise or fall of pitch; for glissandos; for a small raising or lowering of the pitch, such as a half step; and to indicate the conductor's down beat.

19. The height of the stems designates the height of the pitch.

The following examples, taken from school music instructional scores, show several kinds of writing.

Music Example 8–5: David Bedford, *Whitefield Music 1,* for twelve chime-bars, twelve tuned milk bottles, and four drums. Page 1, first four measures quoted.

(This score uses standard pitch symbols.)

Musical Example 8–6: George Self, *Holloway*, for percussion, winds, strings, and piano. First six measures quoted.

4 beats for each bar.

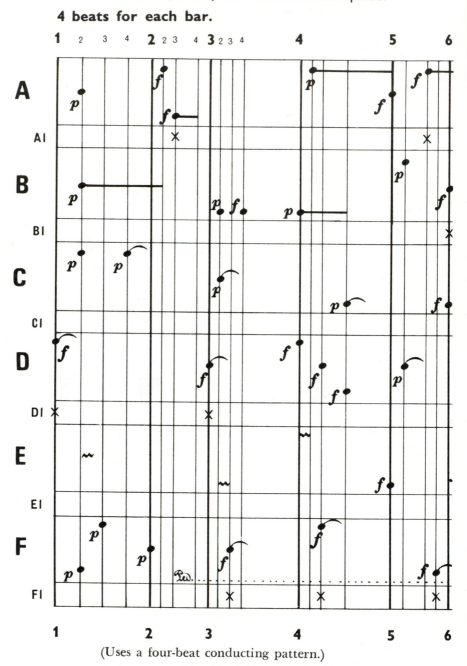

(Uses a four-beat conducting pattern.)

Musical Example 8–7: Brian Dennis, *Tetrahedron*, Instrumental Score with Optional Organ score.

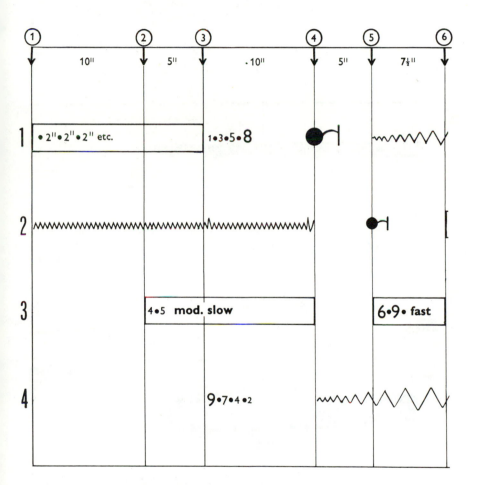

Optional Organ part

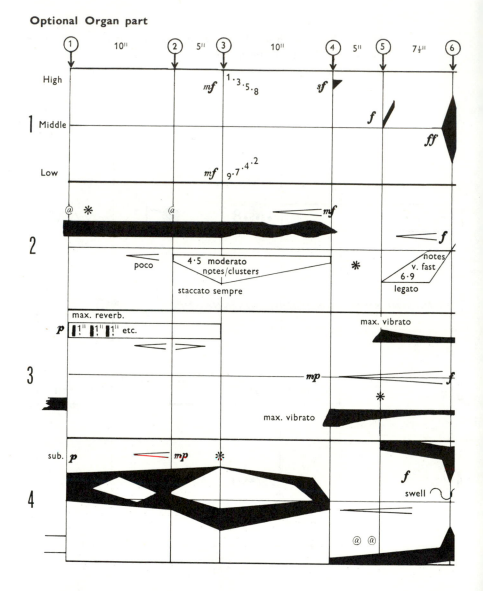

No standard symbols, conductor's "signals" indicated with timing in seconds shown between signals. Composer specifies: any instruments, preferably non-pitched, plus organ (electronic recommended). The instruments in each group should be of similar character and number. First six measures of instrumental score and first six measures of organ score quoted here.

The spaced notation, improvised score sounds, and abstract designing of the score page are all phenomena of the twentieth century. The appearance of the score itself becomes a sort of abstraction. Clarity of musical understanding is necessary for positive action and constructive interpretation. Since the happenings in music of this kind vary somewhat from performance to performance, there is in each rendition a certain lack of permanence built into the work of art. Whether or not such compositions will achieve a permanent place in the concert repertoire is at present an unanswerable question. Only time will tell.

But in the meantime, the up-to-date conductor should familiarize himself with the new mores that are becoming accepted in our long tradition of musical art.

Supplementary Readings *(See Appendix F)*

WILLIAM W. AUSTIN, *Music in the 20th Century,* from Debussy through Stravinsky. (Includes a magnificent bibliography, pp. 552–662.)

D. BEHRMAN, "What Indeterminate Notation Determines." in *Perspectives of New Music,* Spring–Summer, 1965, pp. 58–73.

REGINALD SMITH BRINDLE, *Serial Composition.*

JOHN CAGE, *Notations.*

ROBERT A. CHOATE, BARBARA KAPLAN, and JAMES STANDIFER, *Sound, Beat and Feeling,* pp. 198–199, and *Sound, Shape and Symbol,* pp. 18–21 and 158–159. Both books are from the *New Dimensions in Music Series.* Instructional Materials for the Educator.

DAVID COPE, *New Directions in Music.*

RICHARD L. CROCKER, *A History of Musical Style,* Chapter 16, "New Music after 1900," pp. 483–526.

R. ERICKSON, "Time-Relations," in *Journal of Music Theory,* Winter, 1963, pp. 174–192.

ERHARD KARKOSCHKA, *Das Schriftbild der neuen Musik.* (Even if you cannot read German, this book is worth exploring. The illustrations are most revealing.)

RUTH KOENIG, *Notation in New Music, a critical guide to Interpretation and Realization,* Translated from the German by Ruth Koenig, New York, Praeger, 1972. (A translation of the Karkoschka book.)

GEORGE SELF, *New Sounds in Class, A Contemporary Approach to Music.*

K. STONE, "Problems and Methods of Notation," in *Perspectives of New Music,* Spring, 1963, pp. 9–31.

Exercises for Practice

1. Using the symbols given in Table 8–1, write a composition for several players; get a group together and perform it.
2. Explore the compositions of the composers listed in the text. Note their individual kinds of scores.

chapter **9**

On Teaching Conducting

Green

Teaching conducting is an art in its own right, but only in the twentieth century has it emerged as an exact science, mainly because of the intensive research of Nicolai Malko in this field of endeavor.

As Malko once remarked, "When I found I was to *teach* conducting, then I really had to know cause and effect." His dedicated searching gave him a phenomenal understanding of the psychological and spontaneous responses musicians make to the subtleties of the conductor's motions. And he eventually developed therefrom an exact science.

As we prove year after year in our conducting classes, there are certain gestures that will *never* produce the desired response and there are certain gestures that are foolproof in obtaining specific reactions from the players. A conductor who knows and understands the difference is immediately recognizable.

An anecdote will illustrate. Malko said, "If you look at your French horn when giving this particular cue, you will get a *forte* entrance. But the composer has requested a *piano* here." In the conducting class, the student looked at the horn player, and a *forte* sounded. Upon request from the professor to repeat the passage, the same thing happened. Whereupon the professor, to test Malko's word, took the baton, conducted the passage, looked at the hornist, and again a *forte* sound came forth. Then, once more the professor conducted the passage, this time *not* looking at the player and a beautiful *piano* emerged!

When the professor then explained to the class what was being tested, the horn player burst into a loud guffaw and exclaimed, "Someone has written four P's in big letters under this entrance and I never even saw them until you did not look at me!" This is startling, to say the least. The fact that a previous player had desperately marked four *pianos* under the entrance also proved that a previous conductor had had to scold the previous player for the same *forte* rendition. If the unique danger this entrance entailed had been understood, there would have been no problem.

Although this anecdote illustrates a particular place in a particular score, it also shows Malko's infinite knowledge of his art. The technical gestures of the baton and left hand had been carefully analyzed and thoroughly tested with the great professional orchestras throughout the world. Popular opinion to the contrary, these can be taught and learned just as technique on any sounding instrument is taught and learned.

The baton technique is subtle because it is a technique of *appearance* instead of a technique of *sound*. The conductor develops, through concentrated study and diligent practice, a bi-manual technique similar to that required for stringed instrument playing—the two hands working independently of each other but correlating as necessary. Ivan Galamian, the great violin pedagogue, writes, "The mind, which has to be able to anticipate the action, must have a clear picture of the motion involved, of its technical timing, and of the anticipated sounds in order to give its commands with clarity and precision." . . . "Technique . . . implies the ability to do justice, with unfailing reliability and control, to each and every demand of the most refined musical imagination." [1]

In building technique, it is the link between the mind and hands that has to be strengthened. The mind needs to *know* and then the hands have to *do*. The unfrustrated conductor is in *full control of a knowledgeable technique.*

BUILDING THE CONDUCTING SKILLS

Charles Blackman says, "The primary function of a conductor is communication." [2] This is a powerful and all-encompassing statement. It will bear thought and study.

In all conducting classes, setting up time-beating patterns, presenting score format, and studying the transposing instruments are standard routines. Methodology for these has long been in existence. Here we will consider the order of events in the teaching of conducting technique. Learning to conduct is like learning to drive a car. The driver learns how to start and stop the motion, how to speed up and slow down the motion,

---

[1] Ivan Galamian, *Principles of Violin Playing and Teaching* (Englewood Cliffs, N.J.: Prentice-Hall, Inc., 1962), p. 99 and p. 5. Used by permission.

[2] Charles Blackman, *Behind the Baton* (New York: Charos Enterprises, Inc. [Carl Fischer, Inc., selling agent], 1964), p. 27. Used by permission of Charles Blackman.

how to turn the corners, always keeping the machine under control. In the teaching-learning process, the young conductor needs first to acquire the feeling of handling his "machine." It is necessary for him to find out quickly that he can control the happenings.

The preparatory beat with the subsequent sounding beat, plus the cutting off of the sound, together with its resumption—these are the first steps in *control*. A gesture of cutting off is a demand for a decisive response; a new preparation and a command to play again give the basic elements for the *feeling* of conducting. (A four-beat pattern with the cut-offs coming on various beats, continuing thereafter, makes a fine drill study.)

Once the start-stop-start is functioning, control of the height of the rebound, after the first beat of each measure, should be acquired. This is the first of the *technical* controls. When the first beat of the measure rebounds up to the top, then the second and succeeding beats tend to look like first beats. This is what is meant by ambiguous time beating. The musicians cannot "read the beat," and therefore they perform without leadership, ignoring the conductor's motions and depending on their own mutual musicianship to keep the ensemble together.

And so we come to the easy, natural flexibility of the baton wrist. Since it is most difficult to teach, it is rarely seen in its matured form. In answering a question about time beating from the elbow, the wrist remaining static, Malko replied, "The arm feeling is good, but the wrist must be malleable. Use the physical exercises (see the diagrams at the beginning of *The Conductor and his Baton*),[3] but moving only from the elbow, the hand hanging down as the arm moves upward and vice versa. Many conductors, including Toscanini, *look* as if the whole arm is moving as one rigid unit, but this is deceiving. In reality the wrist is responding: It is not inflexible." (*Note:* This has been confirmed by players who were in the Toscanini orchestras. One player told Malko, "Because it is really relaxed. It is his trick.")

There seems to be a misconception today. "The baton is an extension of the arm" is being misconstrued to mean that the wrist action is to be denied. But the wrist is part of the arm, and only its easy flexibility gives the stick a *musical* appearance. It is true that motion coming from the elbow and delivered to the baton through a rigid or inflexible wrist can acquire an acceptable, rhythmic appearance, but it cannot acquire a musical one.

However, in all of this emphasis on wrist flexibility, one must caution that no flexibility is preferable to an overdone or snakelike wrist

---

[3] Nicolai Malko, *The Conductor and his Baton* (Copenhagen: Wilhelm Hansen Verlag, 1950), "Physical Exercises," pp. 39–51, and "The Left Hand," pp. 251–266.

motion. The latter completely destroys the appearance of rhythmic solidity. Malko's curative follows: "Stress solidity of rhythm, a continuity or steadiness of rhythm. Take a driving rhythm and try *crescendo* and *diminuendo* on a long line of such rhythm. Allow no *accelerando,* no *ritard,* on a long *diminuendo.* In general, concentrate on the simple and basic principles instead of stressing the analytical process."

The young conductor, in his eager intensity, finds himself leaning over toward his players or crouching on the sudden *piano* passages. Knee action is not needed to bring an orchestra down to a fine *piano* dynamic, and it is not necessary to lean toward a player when tossing him his cue. The orchestra will respond beautifully to a commanding and technically skillful baton or left-hand motion. Besides, leaning over presents an ungainly appearance to the audience, and it is musically valueless.

Do not stretch the arm forward. A fully stretched arm can bend from the elbow only in one direction. Most of the necessary elbow motion is denied, since with stretched arms the motion originates of necessity in the shoulder.

When the technique is fully developed, each section of the arm becomes responsive to and controlled by the mind, coming into play as the music demands it and without conscious thought. For example, the use of just the hand and wrist for the *subdivisions* of the beat in the Adagio tempos clarifies the picture for the musicians.

It is difficult for the young conductor to stop the feeling of rhythm within himself when he encounters a *fermata.* He does not feel comfortable with the non-rhythmic lengthening of the note. When outstanding teachers in Europe were asked, "What is the hardest thing for the student?" the reply was often, "The handling of the *fermata.*"

Each hand should develop the skill to beat time well, but the practical use of continuous time beating in both hands simultaneously throughout a performance becomes monotonous. Let us remember that Malko speaks of the "virtuoso left hand," the left hand that is independent of the baton, independent of the rhythmic pulse, and able to contour phrasing smoothly, and to show dynamics and cues in its own right, without being affected by, or repeating, the rhythmic motions of the right hand.

SOME DIRECT QUOTATIONS FROM
MALKO'S TEACHING

"The conductor should breathe deeply, not get short of breath and breathe faster as the music speeds up. There is no conducting without breathing."

"When speaking to the orchestra, let the baton be at rest. Put the hand down. Do not hold the stick in a position of readiness."

Quoting his teacher, Felix Mottl: "You must use *only* the gestures that help the orchestra, not fix the hair nor straighten the cuffs in performance."

"When cutting off a *fermata* there is a danger of too much preparation causing an unpleasant accent as the sound is stopped. Make the cut-off simple and definite, without too much impulse of will."

"In conducting there is a moment of pause *to show intention*. A dog in the path of an automobile—a sudden moment of pause to think what to do. This moment sometimes costs the creature his life. Or a cat with a dish of milk. A dog approaches. A moment of pause while the cat thinks how to deal with the situation."

"Every conductor must use the rhythmic feeling of his players. This feeling of theirs, however, must be arranged first with his own rhythmic feeling."

Malko was holding a conducting class. A student was chewing gum. Malko exclaimed, "Gum! Don't bring gum to a conducting class. You have then two beats—two conductors."

And finally one typical anecdote: Malko, attending a less than adequate lecture, remarked, "Sometimes they should hang the lecturer before the lecture. . . . It would make marvelous publicity."

SOME ANSWERS TO PEDAGOGIC QUESTIONS (MALKO)

What does one do for the timid student?
Answer: Stress first a solid rhythmic approach. Make this the first requisite. Let other things go until this good rhythm is established.

What does one do to cure the too-high rebound after the first beat of the measure?
Answer: Most conductors do it! . . . even the best of them. When I see so many others doing it, I wonder if I do it myself, even when I do not intend to. Nevertheless, even though we may do it, the technique is undeniably better for the orchestra if the rebound is controlled properly. Stress it with students—stress it several times if necessary. If they still do not get it, tell them, "Look! If you do not do it now with all of this emphasis, you probably won't do it when you stand in front of the orchestra. *So get it now!"*

What about memory work?
Answer: Do not stress it artificially. Fear, if built up in the beginning

stages by too soon a demand for memorization, can result in permanent damage. Stress rather a bit of recognition of form-analysis, a by-ear approach, a musical feeling first. . . . Using familiar songs that everyone knows is good as an initial step in scoreless conducting.

What should the teacher do about the student who conducts with emotional tension and becomes stiff and rigid in his motions?

Answer: This is not good—only the *appearance* of the stress must be there, not the stress itself. [Then Malko gave the illustration of a great Russian actor in the role of Othello.] The story was originally related by the actor who played Iago opposite Othello. This actor said, "When Othello lunged for me, to choke me, I *involuntarily* screamed. I truly thought he had forgotten himself and would actually kill me. But when his hands touched my neck, the touch was like a feather." Malko continued, "Only the *appearance* of the tension was there in the actor's hands. Conducting should be like this. When the emotion itself comes into the action, then the action does not always show what it is supposed to show. Instead it often becomes unrhythmic."

What does one do when the players are too responsive to the baton, exaggerating the effects?

Answer: Sometimes just withdrawing a bit from the orchestra will take care of the situation. Retract the hands a bit. For the section of the orchestra at your left, bring the vertical gestures more to the right, and so on.

And finally, what about the student who is really talented, full of music and full of leadership, but lax on technique?

Answer: You cannot harness genius. Ask him, "This is difficult for you, yes? But just because you do it adequately now, this is no excuse for your not acquiring a really good technique which will enable you to do it still better. Your results will improve as your technique improves. With such a student be absolutely merciless if necessary. *His talent demands it!"*

Appendixes

APPENDIX A: Review of Transpositions

THE TWO BASIC RULES FOR TRANSPOSITION

Rule I. To find out how the part actually *sounds:*

1. Write the note C, third space, treble clef.
2. Next to it write the key name of the instrument as stated in the left margin of the score (B-flat, A, F, etc.).
3. This gives the interval of transposition.
4. Every note of the written part must pass through that interval when played on the piano; in other words, to get to its sounding pitch.

Note: Transposition instruments are all in the treble clef. In applying Rule I, all transpositions go downward except as follows:

Trumpets in D, E-flat, E-natural, and F (upward)

E-flat soprano clarinet (upward) (see page 136).

Rule II. When the part has to be played on an instrument other than the one for which it was originally written:

1. Write the key name of the instrument *to be played on.*
2. Next to that write the name of the instrument originally called for in the score, the instrument for which the part was originally written.
3. This gives the interval of this transposition.
4. The instrument now playing the part must throw every note through that interval in order to arrive at the correct sound.

Caution: Note that the French horns were built in the following keys:

(B♭ Basso)

In applying Rule II, when horn in D is called for, remember that it is the D below the staff that must be written. All horns go downward from the C.

Trumpets were built in the following keys:

Trumpets in D, E-flat, E-natural, and F go upward from the C.

Several drill sheets for the application of these two rules are found on the following pages.

See the complete listing of instruments in Table A–1.

Instruments in C sound as notated; sometimes an octave higher or lower. See Table A–1.

Transpositions: Set I

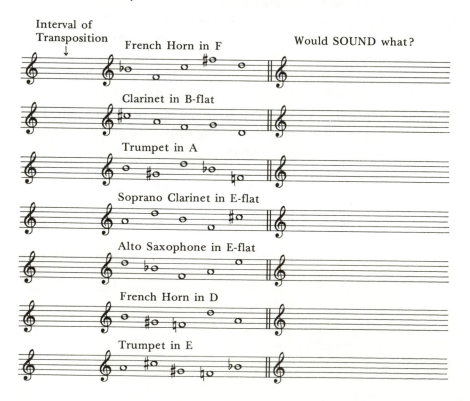

Interval of Transposition

French Horn in F   Would SOUND what?

Clarinet in B-flat

Trumpet in A

Soprano Clarinet in E-flat

Alto Saxophone in E-flat

French Horn in D

Trumpet in E

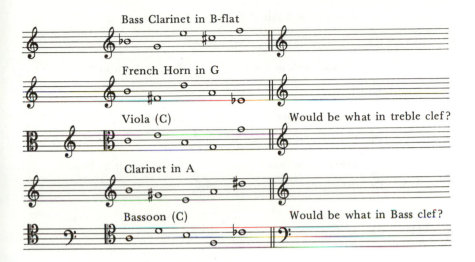

Transpositions: Set II

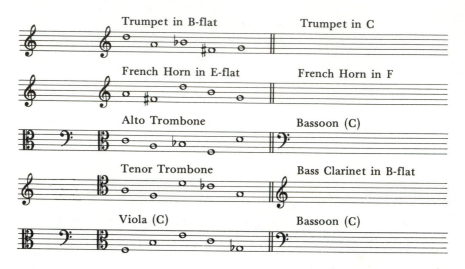

Table A–1: **Instruments**

Written Part Sounds:

Piccolo in C
  (up an octave)
Piccolo in D-flat
  (up a major ninth)
Flute in C
Oboe in C
English horn in F
  (down a perfect fifth)
Clarinet in B-flat
  (down a major second)
Clarinet in A
  (down a minor third)
Soprano clarinet in E-flat
  (up a minor third)
Alto clarinet in F, Basset horn
  (down a perfect fifth)
Alto clarinet in E-flat
  (down a major sixth)
Bass clarinet in B-flat
  (down a major ninth)
Bass clarinet in E-flat
  (down an octave plus a major sixth)

Bassoon in C
Contrabassoon in C
  (down an octave)
French horn in F
  (down a perfect fifth)
The following horns all sound down-
  ward from C (third space): B-flat, A,
  A-flat, G, F, E, E-flat, D, C-basso,
  B-flat basso
Trumpet or cornet in B-flat
  (down a major second)
Trumpet in C
Trumpets in D, E-flat, E-natural and F,
  all go upward from third-space C
Trumpet in A
  (down a minor third)
Trombones (alto, tenor)
  (as written)
Bass trombone
  (down an octave)
Baritone in B-flat, treble clef
  (down a major ninth)
  bass clef, as written

Strings: violin, viola, cello
(as written)

String bass
(down an octave)

Soprano saxophone in B-flat
(down a major second)

Alto saxophone in E-flat
(down a major sixth)

Tenor saxophone in B-flat
(down a major ninth)

Baritone saxophone in E-flat
(down an octave plus a major sixth)

Bass saxophone in B-flat
(down an octave plus a major ninth)

Contrabass saxophone in B-flat
(an octave below bass saxophone)

Tubas, as written in bass clef

Chimes in C

Glockenspiel in C
(up two octaves)

Xylophone in C
(up an octave)

Celesta in C
(up an octave)

Timpani
(as notated)

Harp, as written

APPENDIX B: Review of Harmonics and Stringed Instrument Tone Colors

Stringed instrument harmonics are either natural or artificial. The natural harmonic is played by touching the string lightly at exactly one-half, one-third, one-fourth, one-fifth, etc., of its length. In so doing the string breaks itself automatically into segments (two, three, four, or five). The division points of the segments are called *nodes*. The resultant sound follows the "chord of nature" series and is ethereal in sound.

> The Chord of Nature Series:
> Fundamental (the open string).
> The octave harmonic—uses half the string.
> The fifth above the octave harmonic—uses one-third of the string.
> Two octaves above the fundamental—uses one-fourth of the string.
> Two octaves plus the major third—string in five parts.
> Two octaves plus a perfect fifth—string in six parts.
> Two octaves plus the minor seventh—string in seven parts (sounds flat).
> Three octaves—string in eight parts.

On the violin and viola we seldom use the harmonics in this form beyond the division into five parts (one-fifth of the string).

To break the string into half, the composer writes the octave of the open string, with a zero above the note.

To break the string into three parts, a diamond-shaped note is used, at an interval of a perfect fifth above the open string.

To break the string into four parts, the note is written a perfect fourth above the open string (diamond-shaped note).

To break the string into five parts, the diamond-shaped note may be written either at a major third or a major sixth above the open string.

When the composer wishes the player to use the node nearest the bridge (the hand being in a high position), he writes the note at actual pitch in normal notation (not diamond-shaped) and places the zero above it.

The artificial harmonics are formed by placing the first finger (or thumb in cello and bass) solidly on the string on the desired pitch, and then touching the same string lightly with the little finger (or third finger in cello and bass). In this way, any pitch on the instrument may be turned into a harmonic sound. Since the interval between first and fourth fingers (or thumb and third finger) is usually a perfect fourth, the resultant harmonic sound will be two octaves above the given pitch (the pitch on which the first finger or thumb rests). This is the easiest way for the player to perform the artificial harmonics. The note under the first finger (or thumb) is written in regular notation, but the fourth above, fingered by the small finger (or third finger) is written as a diamond-shaped note.

On violin and viola it is possible to stretch the little finger one whole step above its normal position. When this is done, the resultant harmonic sound will be an octave and a fifth above the solidly fingered note. It is, however, more clumsy for the player.

In performing harmonics the bow should be used close to the bridge, with sufficient pressure to insure a good tone. In this way it does not interfere with the formation of the nodes.

When the score calls for *ponticello* (Italian), *am Steg* (German), or *sur le chevalet* (French), it signifies that the bow is to be used near the bridge with a faster, lighter stroke. The resultant tone color is a shimmering sound that combines the harmonic sound with the fundamental.

Tone colors are varied on the stringed instruments by the distance of the bow from the bridge. When the bow is moving on a nodal point, that harmonic cannot be sounded. It therefore disappears from the resultant tone color.

APPENDIX C: Score Excerpts and Solutions to Problems

Music Example A-1: Dvořák, Slavonic Dance, Op. 72, No. 3 At Letter G. (Sixteen measures from the end) *Più animato.*

Music Example A-2: Mahler, Symphony No. 5. in C-sharp minor. First movement, "Funeral March," measures 1-60. "In measured tempo. Strict. Like a funeral march."

★ Vorschläge so schnell als möglich.

Music Example A-3: Dvořák, Slavonic Dance. Op. 72. No. 3 Measures 15-38.
Allegro.

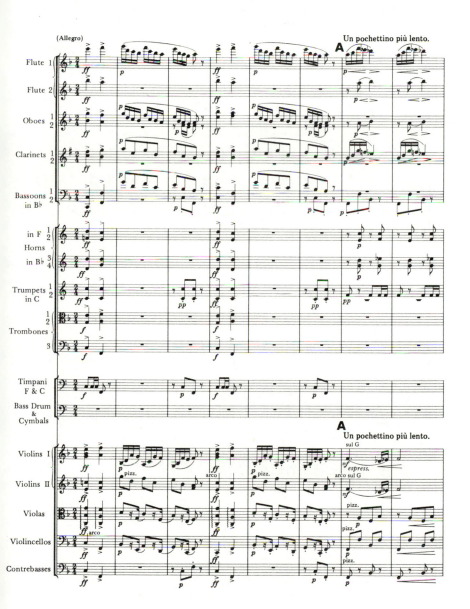

Music Example A-4: Bach-Abert: Prelude, Chorale, and Fugue. (Published by Kalmus.) Fugue only, quoted here. Measures 1-59.

Note: This excerpt is chosen for the many facets of score-memorization illustrated in these opening measures. Apply the markings from Chapters 3 and 4. Edit as outlined on page 76, first marking in the instrumentation where missing, then doing the phrasing. Use the bracket for the Fugue-theme entrances.

Problem: For Applying Memorization Techniques

Suggested Solutions for Page 11

1. Check immediately to see if there is a misprint in the player's part.
2. Check the height of your rebound after the first beat of each measure. When it climbs too high, beat Two looks like another beat One. Confusing!
3. Soften the accompanying parts, or cut down on the number of players on each of those parts.
4. Obviously you are stopping every few measures to talk to the players. Play farther before stopping, thus giving the musical line a chance to form. Wait until the players have become involved with the music itself. See page 95, last paragraph.
5. Check on the number of measures of rest in the player's part preceding his entrance. There may be a misprint. Pay attention to the possible need for a cue in such places. Give it!

Suggestions Regarding the Phrasing

1. MAHLER: A cursory glance might give the impression that the phrasing is entirely in four-measure groupings. Try this:

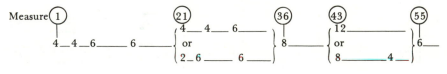

2. DVOŘÁK: 3_3_5__4_5__5__.
3. BACH: Here you are on your own.

Facets of Memorization Illustrated by the Bach Fugue Excerpt

All of these are useful in the right place, at the right time, when memorizing score in order to conduct.

The Several Techniques Used:

    a. Melody (themes) recognition. Here, the Fugue theme.
    b. Measure counting for security in dangerous places. See 1 and 5 below.
    c. Contours of passages leading to cues: 2, 3, 6 below.
    d. Pitch recognition of warning notes: 2, 3, 6 below.
    e. Alternation of instruments on motifs or phrases: 4 below.
    f. Motif or short-phrase recognition, repeated: 7 below.

For Memorizing: *First, Analyze the Form; Then Mark the Phrasing.*

1. Measures 1-6. Count the measures to the second fugue entrance. Think: "Entrance after Two in the sixth measure," second violins.
2. Measures 14-18. The runs in violin I *ascend* (measures 17-18) to the first high G. Entrance after Two, violas and cellos.
3. Measures 26-27. The half-note syncopations *descend* in violin I. The entrance is after Two when the *second* high G is sounded, cellos and basses.
4. Letter A, measure 34 and continuing. Alternation of cellos plus basses against first and second violins. Entrances are after Two. The cue for continuing is the two quarter notes in the second violins in measure 42. It is the only measure throughout the alternation section that has quarter notes on One. Fugue entrance after Two, violin I.
5. Measures 43-48. Same as measures 1-6. Violin II in sixth measure, after Two.
6. Measures 54-57. Flute descends in tied-over half-notes to letter B. First entrance of the trombone ON Two of the flute's last scale-note, D. Cellos and basses must know to enter immediately after the trombones. The cue is addressed to the trombones. Note that they are playing the initial four-measure phrase of the Chorale theme.

End of excerpt

APPENDIX D: Outline Notes on Repertoire

The outlines in this appendix identify, by measure, technical and interpretative facets of the conducting as stressed by Malko.

Beethoven, Symphony No. 1 in C Major, fourth movement.

The repeats are good in both the first and last movements.

In the introduction to the fourth movement, show the staccato and legato effects as indicated by the composer.

Measure 1: Use the preparatory breathing gesture before the initial fermata, ff. Cut to the right and prepare Four.

Measure 6: Cut the fermata again to the right. The cut-off gesture may be considered as One of the Allegro tempo, followed immediately by Two in the baton, Allegro; or, the fermata may be completely cut off, the caesura observed, and followed by a One (in Allegro) in the left hand with the Two in the baton after which the violins enter on their three sixteenth notes.

Measures 79–85: Use the gesture of syncopation on the first beat of each measure.

Measures 96–105: Note the three runs in the first violins, *piano,* but on measure 106, the pp dynamic should be observed.

Measure 108 (thirteenth measure after the double bar—ff): Use the tenuto gesture.

Measures 109–110: Staccato gestures.

Measures 112 and following: Legato gestures.

Measure 130: Bring out the syncopes in the woodwinds.

Measures 160–161: Staccato *forte.*

Measure 162: Marked *piano,* but really should be mf-dim-*piano.* Just be sure that in *piano* it *sounds.* If the mf-*piano* is used, it will still sound *forte-piano* to the audience and everything will be heard clearly.

Measure 235: Cut the fermata to the left and upward. The baton is then ready to come down into the first beat of the next measure immediately. There is no space between this first fermata and what follows.

Measure 237: Hold the fermata to the right, thus preparing the baton for the second beat in this measure. This second beat follows immediately upon the heels of the long-sustained sound of the fermata. It states Two as a cut-off for the fermata and simultaneously as a beat for the violins to continue the music.

Measures 238–242: Note the three runs *piano,* two runs in *double-piano,* and then *piano* again. The *piano-beat* then continues until measure 246 when the sudden *forte* enters.

Measure 258: The sudden *forte* again (ff).

Last eight measures: Beat only the first beat in each measure (seven first beats); then hold the hands in position long enough for the last measure of rest. Show that you really need that measure to complete your picture.

Beethoven, Symphony No. 5 in C Minor.

The up beat at the beginning should be rhythmic, and staccato.

First beat, double-forte in One.

Fermata, unmetrical.

Cut-off of the fermata to the right, continuing into the down beat of the next measure.

Down beat for the third measure immediately. No long wait.

Second fermata, show *two* beats, the first for the measure before the fermata, and the second for the fermata itself.

Measure 57: The dead gesture.

Measure 65 and following: Don't forget the cello and bass cues here.

Measures 123 and 124: Dead gestures.

Measures 196 and following: Tenuto gesture until the *double-forte* on the first beat of measure 228.

Second Movement:

Set the tempo by characteristic passages as in measures 98–99.

Third Movement:

The up beat at the beginning is a whole measure with the orchestra entering on the last one-third of the measure. The down beat is the second note of the cellos and basses.

Measure 7: Indicate the last quarter note of this measure (to handle the *poco ritard* indicated by the composer).

Measure 8: The cut-off of the fermata is made upward, similarly to the preparatory beat at the beginning, the cellos entering thereafter and the conductor meeting them on the following down beat (One of the next measure).

Beethoven, *Egmont* Overture

Give this composition a tragic character throughout. "Even the themes are tragic."

Note: Horn in D drops the seventh: trumpets in D go up one tone: the same writing for these two sounds an octave apart.

Measure 1: Breathing gesture, *forte,* diminuendo.

Measure 2: Tenuto, marcato. Expect the half notes to be quarter notes here. Remember that in early writing the dot beside the note added half the value of the note, but above or below the note it subtracted half the value.

Measure 8: The swell-dim is important here.

Measure 15 and following: Pay attention to horns, bassoons, celli and basses.

Allegro (starts on measure 25).

Measure 25: In three beats, with the one-beat structure starting even on the second measure.

Measures 28–29: Celli, sf crescendo into the D and back down to the C, not sfp on the first C.

Measures 47–58: A long crescendo, steady tempo.

Measure 74 and following: Sf, then tenuto.

Measure 82: In Three, staccato.

Measure 84: In One, legato (this pattern continues as in measures 82 and 84).

Measure 92 and following: In One.

Measure 100: Wrist accent on Three.

Measure 110 and following: Tenuto after the accent.

Measure 123 and following: Beat first and third beats with the third beat accenting in the baton wrist for the *forte* chords when they occur *or* beat One and Two and stop the baton and the orchestra will carry the two accented chords correctly.

Measure 162 and following: Same as measures 28–29.

Recapitulation: Same as exposition.

Allegro con brio:

Editor's note: *Malko does not cut off before the first note of the Allegro. The last note of the preceding section is held very softly and sneaks right into the Allegro. It makes a great effect.*

Measure 287: Begin in Four; go to Two at measure 295.

Measure 291–294: Crescendo.

Measure 295: Sustain the brass in this figure in the long notes—a full-throated swell.

Measure 307: In Four for eight (or ten) measures.

Measure 329 and following: Don't let the tone die after the sf here.

Measure 338: Don't hurry the octave skips here.

Haydn, Symphony No. 104 in D Major (London).

First Movement

Adagio: It is all right to use the divided beat until the fermata, then just sustain this note and keep the *forte* character. Don't make a long pause after the fermata.

Measure 6: Don't hurry the last eighth note.

Measures 7–8: Beat out slightly the half notes where there is no fermata.

The fermata just before the Allegro could have been written on the barline. Haydn insures its being long enough by putting in the quarter rest.

Note: Begin counting measures from the Allegro from here on.

Measures 2–3: Insure the staccato here.

Measures 24 and 26: Sf-tenuto on the first beat.

Measure 29 and following: Remind strings of the staccato here, possibly with the left hand.

Measures 38–39: Insure the sf here.

Measure 48: Do not relax the interest on the second beat. Keep hands poised for the next part.

Measure 64 and following: Note the three-measure, two-measure, one-measure construction here.

Measures 74–75: Very broadly tenuto.

Measures 76, 77, 78, 79: Gesture of syncopation on the first beat of each measure to aid the sf on the second quarter note.

Measure 83: Finish ff on the first beat. Don't look at your horns here or they will sfp their note. Leave them alone and they will play the *piano* well.

Measures 83–84: Staccato for the second violins and viola: then legato for the first violins and flute in measure 85.

Measures 96 and 100, 101: Gesture of syncopation on the first beat for the sf effect on the syncopated beat.

Measure 107: Keep the interest here on the rest, same as in measure 48.

Measures 108–109: Observe the crescendo-diminuendo in the first violins.

Measure 115 and following: Indicate the staccato for the quarter notes in the baton for the violas, cellos, and basses if they are to your right, and in the left hand for the flutes and oboes. Observe the legato notes in both sections by a change of character in the hand controlling that section.

Measure 121 and following: Same.

Measure 176: Don't relax after this climax. Don't let the players ever be completely at ease during the fermata on the rest. Audience may clap here if you do. Let hands rebound to a position of readiness after the first beat.

Measure 200: Tenuto gesture on first beat.

Measures 226–227: One dead gesture only on the first beat of each measure. Do not beat out the second beat.

Recapitulation: The same as the exposition.

Last measure of the piece: Keep up the interest and quality on the last note. Be sure you beat the last note exactly the same as the two preceding notes.

Second Movement (Andante)

In Four

Note: Legato, staccato, dead gestures on rests, sf-tenuto and staccato in the first three measures. Use this first repeat.

Measure 6: Observe the crescendo-diminuendo in the lower strings.

Measures 22, 23, 24: Pay attention to the *crescendo* to *forte* followed by the *diminuendo.*

Measure 25: Hold the *fermata* long and softly.

Measure 27: Breadth and *forte* on the *tenuto.*

Measure 34: Sixteenths in two-note slurs, espressivo on the first note of each slur. "First note always a little longer than the second in this figure."

Measure 37: Don't use this repeat. "This symphony is long (not in time but in *material*), and it is better to omit this repeat."

Measure 55: Keep the interest and the *double-forte* clear through this measure.

Measure 56: One dead gesture for the measure; don't wait too long before making this gesture.

Measure 70: FORTE!

Measure 74 and following: Same as beginning.

Measure 89: Hands in readiness during the *fermata*.

Measure 117: Slight *ritard* and a delayed last note in the flute.

Measure 149: Horns *a tempo* with a slight slackening of speed in the second measure (measure 150).

Schubert, Symphony No. 8 in B Minor (Unfinished)

First Movement (Note the "phrasal conducting," first 8 measures.)

The up beat takes the time of one beat (preparatory beat).

Measure 1: Indicate only the first beat of the first measure and sustain.

Measure 2: Indicate the first and third beats.

Measure 3: First beat only and sustain.

Measure 4: Beat all three beats.

Measure 5: Show the first and third beats.

Measures 6, 7: First beat only.

Measure 8: Show first beat and then the third beat legato to indicate coming tempo for the violins.

Measure 9: Time-beating as such starts here. Use the left hand for "together" and "rhythm" in cellos and basses.

Measure 13: Long line of clarinet-oboe melody, legato beat.

Measure 38: First gesture sf, second gesture *forte*.

Measures 39–40: One beat in each measure.

Measure 41: Three beats.

Measure 44: Espressivo in baton—celli soli.

Measure 53: Same for the violins.

Measure 62: Dead gesture for the first beat of the measure and then just wait for the other beats to pass.

Measure 63: Ff first beat, legato-diminuendo motion for the rest of the measure and tenuto on the first beat of measure 64. Do not beat out the rest of this measure, but prepare for the next measure.

Measure 71: Fz forte on beat One. Do not prepare the *diminuendo* in the woodwinds until after the first beat.

Measures 73–76: Legato, then *forte-staccato* on 77.

Measure 85: Sf on second beat of measure; then combine the third beat with the second to form one gesture.

Measure 106 and following: Don't beat time. Indicate the pizzicato notes with the left hand, the baton remaining quiescent. Prepare each note.

Measure 124: Indicate the viola entrance.

Measure 134: Use the wrist accent for all trombone notes.

Measure 176: Concentrate on the running figure (violins) so that it sounds against the main theme.

Measure 186: See that the violins sustain the *forte* on this note.

Measures 208–210 and following: Prepare the third beat for the strings.

Measure 332: Eyes to the French horns and woodwinds for preparation.

Measures 364–366: Give only the first beat of the measure. Last note a tenuto gesture and stop conducting. Retract the hands *immediately* after the tenuto gesture.

Schubert, *Rosamunde* Overture.

(Taken directly from one of Malko's letters.)

In this overture, differentiate between the sf and the fp (ffp). The latter have a quasi melodic sense: *f-dim-p,* rather than fp.

In measure 33, Schubert writes ff $\Longrightarrow$ p, and in the 34th bar fz or fz $\Longrightarrow$ p. But in both bars the dynamic meaning is the same. Perhaps in the 33rd bar ff $\Longrightarrow$ and in the 34th bar, f $\Longrightarrow$. The same in bar 36. In all of these cases do not force the gesture. It is better to receive a smaller *forte* than to spoil the line by jerking it. In such cases I use a broad gesture, not a small jerky one.

At the beginning do not break the continuity of the half note by using sharp gestures, but instead a soft marking of the second and third beats can help. Be careful in using the third beat as a preparation—otherwise they will play a half note followed by a quarter rest in each case. The length of the first fermata—not quite two bars, either a bit shorter or a bit longer. The second fermata, longer; in any case, longer than two bars. (Count it out if you wish.)

Measure 16: I doubt if it could be played as written because then you will hear sf instead of *forte-piano*. Better do it like this:

Strings:

On the second measure, no crescendo before the *forte*. Take just a bit of time.

Woodwinds:

No accent. It will be too sharp.

Use f ══════ p.

Very important (and beautiful) is the *decrescendo* in the seventeenth bar (and in bar 31). And it is right to use tenuto or even legato gestures in all cases like bars 16 and 17. Otherwise, one cannot preserve the moving line. But not too slowly. The limit is a quarter note at 50, no slower!

My advice is to conduct all of this introduction with rather broad gestures, not changing the gesture too much; for me that means nuances more from the wrist without breaking the general type of time beating.

J. Strauss, *Tales of the Vienna Woods.*

(Taken directly from a letter by Malko.)

I am giving here the approximate scale of tempo but . . . be careful! Do not consider these tempos obligatory.

Beginning: Quarter note at 132.

From the 12th bar: Quarter note at 144 to 152.

From bar 40: Poco animato, quarter note at 152–160.

Bars 54–55: A little *en dehors* (French for "out in front") to mark the horns and trumpets, *quasi ritenente.*

Bar 57: Langsam, very freely: quarter note at 72–100.

Bar 75: Moderato, quarter note at 92 with improvisation of the tempo. For instance, bar 82 *poco* forward to the 83rd bar (quarter note at 120), again *ritard* in bar 86. *Ritard* and *dolcissimo* in 91–92–93.

Bar 94: Poco mosso, more in 96 and 97, a tempo 98, *ritard* in 100. After the second beat in bar 101 a *caesura* (very, very short) and repeat the whole bar in the next tempo (101) thus:

Vivace

Quarter at 112   (♩. = 72)

Editor's note: By "repeat the whole bar" Malko speaks to the conductor: Think *the bar in the new tempo after the* caesura *in order to insure the* vivace.

Bar 110: Very precisely, quarter at 160. Tempo di valse. In the figure of two-eighths-plus-half note, tenuto the half note; do not break it with the gesture Three.

From the Valse (four bars before Waltz I)—the dancing tempo. Something like a quarter note at 152–144, sometimes even 184, mostly trying to do it in One (in character and in gesture).

In *"etwas zuruckhaltend"* (a little ritarded) bar 32 of this waltz, it would be very difficult to do it as written (ritard four bars). Usually it is *a tempo* until the beginning of the 32nd bar, then:

(31)   (32) *poco meno   a tempo* at 138   (34) | (35) |

Quarter at 112   (36) *animato* at 168

And still beginning from Waltz I, be careful with the changing of the tempo. It is important to keep a steady movement in dancing music. Some of my tempos are rather slower than faster. I don't want to write more about tempos so as not to spoil the character of the waltz.

Editor's note: The one place where Malko condoned the use of the up ictus (the beat-point coming at the top of the rebound of the beat) was in conducting waltzes. Each beat acquires the feeling of tossing a ball into the air instead of bouncing it on the ground. This kind of time beating can become vicious as a basic habit and confusing, generally, to the players, but in the waltz it gives a lilt and charm to the sound that is hard to duplicate in any other way. Usually the players do not know what has caused the lilt, but they recognize the difference in sound and musicality of their performance.

Tchaikovsky, Romeo and Juliet Overture Fantasy

It is practical to start out with the first measure in Four. From the second measure on, use Two for phrasing.

At the first double bar the flute and clarinet form an ascending scale on alternate measures: flute, F; clarinet, G-flat; flute, A-flat; clarinet, B-flat, sustained over the bar-line and picked up by the flute in the second half of the second measure; clarinet, C; next measure flute on D-natural, E-natural, and then to high A-flat. Bringing out this ascending scale makes a lovely effect.

> *Editor's note: This scale passage is often overlooked because of the transposition problems of the clarinet part. Often the scale is not clearly heard, as Malko implies. The scale passage comes in again starting in measure 61, but this time it is in the first and second violins, instruments of equal power and tone quality, and it is usually clearly heard. To bring it through in the flute-clarinet combination, it is necessary to rehearse these two instruments alone until they match dynamic and projection equally. And it is, as Malko says, "a lovely effect."*

Measures 28–37: Mind the mf, p, ppp on the successive introductions to the harp chords.

Measure 41: Tenuto for the flute.

Measure 61: The ascending scale in the first and second violins.

Measure 80 and following: Make the *accelerando* and take the *alla breve* at measure 86.

Measure 95: Poco ritard in the third horn leading into the *meno.*

Measure 105: Simply hold out the woodwinds; don't beat it out. *Stringendo* in two beats per measure.

Allegro giusto

Measure 112: First measure of the *allegro giusto* and following: Use the gesture of syncopation on the third beat of these measures and on similar passages throughout.

Measure 118: Show the second beat for the entrance of the tutti, excepting the first violins.

Measure 143: Cymbals!

Measure 143 and following: Starting with measure 142, beat only the "percussion"—the rhythm chords. The runs in the strings will carry themselves. *Prepare* the gesture when the chord comes *on* the beat. Use the gesture of syncopation with its preceding stop for all chords that come *off* the beat, i.e., on the afterbeat.

Measure 150: "Kick" the chord on the second beat.

Measure 151: Watch out! Cymbals on the *third* beat.

Measure 184: In Two for the English horn melody.

Measure 213: Press the tone for the horn. (Tenuto pressure in the baton hand.)

Measure 245: Cue the bassoon.

Measure 251: Cue the second bassoon.

Measure 272: Hold the violas. Show only a small down beat for their second measure of sustaining.

Measure 273: Small gestures for the *allegro* here, and keep them small because of the inability to "encompass" the many instruments of the orchestra in this developmental section. It will get away from you if you don't!

Measure 280: Indicate the second violin entrance after the third beat here.

Measure 285: "Let it ride" on the syncopations; indicate the fourth beat for the brass, etc.

Measure 293: Indicate the horn entrances.

Measure 296: Indicate the woodwinds.

Measure 330: On the *next measure* comes the entrance of the trumpet in E, plus the cymbal crash. Note that this passage is introduced by three *consecutive* runs in the first violins. A complicated passage now begins. Sometimes it is good to have words to think, for example, "After the trumpets . . . after the trumpets," to remind the conductor of the cello entrance on Three.

Measure 331: Compare this rhythmically with the theme as first stated in measure 112. In 112, the gesture of syncopation comes on the third beat; in measure 331, the fourth beat is the important one and must be prepared after Three.

Measure 335: Here one can conduct either the trumpet or the rhythm or use the baton for the trumpet and the left hand for the rhythm. Tenuto for the trumpet.

Measure 388: Horn broader here.

Measure 419: In Four for the violins until the third beat; celli soli can be in Two.

Note: When cellos are in treble clef, they will sound an octave *lower*.

Measures 429–430: Entrances on the third beats: horn; then flute, oboe, and clarinet.

Measure 450: In Two, tenuto.

Measure 463: Cymbals on Four!

Measure 467: Steady and solid in Four.

Measure 471: Chord on Three. *Give it!*

Measure 481: Bowing is Down, Down: In Two tenuto.

Measure 482: Give the fourth beat for the eighth note. In some editions this is printed as a sixteenth note. The eighth is better.

Measure 483: Timpani, start with a slower reiteration of stroke. A slow broad stroke, and increase the speed of alternation as the roll progresses, diminuendo to piano. Makes a fine effect.

Measure 484: After the fermata, prepare the timpani. Give a legato preparatory gesture and keep the tenuto gesture throughout the passage.

Measure 485: Here the tuba is traditionally played an octave *lower.* Have him breathe in the middle of measures 485, 488, 490, and *nowhere else.* In this way the break in the sustained tone will not be noticed.

Measure 494: Don't beat out the beats. Show the beginning of each note.

Measure 510: Cello-bass entrance on Two together with violins.

Measure 518: Do not force the timpani on this *crescendo.* A *forte,* or even an mf, is sufficient in measure 518. But get the ff and permit *no diminuendo* in measure 521. A ff throughout is very grueling on the player.

Measures 519–20: Tenuto the fourth beat, ending it with a gesture of syncopation on One of each following measure.

Editor's note: This example is a fine lesson on how a conductor thinks. It shows the many facets of attention to details: score knowledge, interpretation, knowledge of the "tricks of the trade" for the individual instruments, attention to gesture as a means of reminding the players of the musical qualities of the performance.

von Weber, Oberon Overture.

The fermatas should be *longer* than just the written value of the note.
String entrances in Eight.

Measures 6 and 7: A very slight legato on the first note of the woodwind runs (32nd notes). Felix Mottl said, "It could almost be an effect of rit. accel. rit for these runs."

Measure 9: Tenuto gesture of the last quarter note.

Measure 22: Keep the adagio feeling during the rests and fermatas in this measure.

Measure 24: Tenuto gesture on the quarter note. Let the fourth beat come a little late if necessary. Same wherever this occurs.

Measure 32: Staccato.

Measures 39–40: Tenuto on the accented notes.

Measures 41–42: Tenuto on woodwind and brass quarter notes. Bring out these notes.

Measure 55: French horns, *not* forte-piano, but piano-cresc. The fp effect will sound anyway because of the forte in the strings on the first beat of the measure.

Measure 57: Bowing between the middle and point of the bow, not spiccato. When spiccato is used here, it does not come off together.

Measure 61 and following: Two beats per measure. Resume four-beat pattern on measure 79.

Measure 117 and following: In Two for six measures; show fourth beat on last note of measure 122.

Measure 141: In Two, with first beat subdivided if you wish.

Measure 164: Beat the measure out.

Measure 202: Diminuendo to mf and then crescendo.

Measure 182 and following: Here there are two possible interpretations.

Interpretation A	Interpretation B (Malko preferred this one)
Measure 182: Slight ritard. Slower at measure 183. A tempo at measure 191 and same to the end (or *very slightly* faster).	*Measure 182:* Ritardando, but a tempo at measure 183.
	Measure 191: Take the slower tempo *here;* make a very rigid rhythm in brasses and woodwinds, violas, and cellos.
	Let tempo gradually accelerando all the way to the end. No ritard at all, even in the last two measures. Keep this mad rush up clear to the end. "Fine effect."

Note: in measures 209 and 210:

Don't forget to rewrite the French horns 1 and 2, to double the clarinets: Horn in D:

A FEW WORDS ON STYLE (MALKO)

Mendelssohn, Symphony No. 4 in A Major (Italian).

The style here, in the first movement, is an exaggeration of accents and important beats, and then almost negligible as to width of motions for the light sections. This is a movement of cues. In general in the repertoire it is not good for a conductor to conduct only for cues, but in this first movement they are the important thing.

Mendelssohn's music is like a mosaic. Each part has to fit exactly into place. Therefore, in this movement, first conduct for cues and then superimpose the expression.

French style: *(Editor's note, following one of Malko's performances.) Keep the beat in evidence. Then add and subtract "clever" expression. Remember the humorous touch at the end of the* Iberia Suite *(delicate, like a Frenchman twirling his moustache!) It produced a giggle from the audience as the last note was played.*

APPENDIX E: Malko Biographical Material and Critical Press Notices

CHRONOLOGY

1883: Born, May 4, Brailov, The Ukraine
Father: Andre Malko, a Ukrainian medical doctor
Mother: Olga Petrov, a Russian woman—fine pianist

1883–90: Lived in the village of Semaki in the Ukraine in the house once occupied by Tchaikovsky. Began piano study with mother.

1890: Moved to Odessa. Studied French horn with D. D. Dmitriev and piano with Lagler at the Lagler School. Played timpani in an orchestra conducted by his father, Dr. Malko.

1902: Entered the Conservatory at St. Petersburg. Also enrolled in the University of St. Petersburg for the academic work.

1906: Graduated from the University in History.

1908: Hired, while still a student at the Conservatory, to conduct at the Imperial Theater (Mariinsky Theater) in St. Petersburg.

1909: Graduated from the Conservatory in Composition and Conducting, having been under the instruction of Rimsky-Korsakoff, Glazounow, and Liadov.

1910: Summer, sent to Germany to study conducting with Felix Mottl.

1911: Summer, returned to Germany for further study with Mottl.

1917: Conducted ballet at the Mariinsky Theater on the night of the Revolution—no knowledge of the Revolution until the next morning.

1918: To Vitebsk where he taught and conducted for four years.

1922: To Moscow; organized and taught the conducting classes at the Moscow Conservatory.

1925: To St. Petersburg (Leningrad) as Professor of Conducting and Orchestra at the Conservatory.

1926: Added the duties of Administrative Director and Chief Conductor, Leningrad Philharmonic Orchestra.

1929: Toured South America as guest conductor.

1930: Began his years as Guest Conductor, Copenhagen (Denmark) State Radio Orchestra.

1932: Became "Permanent Guest Conductor" (two–three months each year) in Copenhagen.

1936–37: Taught at the Salzburg Summer Symposium for Conductors.
1940: To the United States: Guest Conductor, Boston Symphony and NBC Symphony of the Air; Also CBS.
1940 and 1941: Summers, conducted at Ravinia (Chicago Symphony).
1941–42: Conductor of the Chicago Women's Symphony.
1943: Mexico City.
1944, 1945, 1946: Guest Conductor at Salt Lake City.
1944, 1945, 1946: Grant Park Summer Concerts in Chicago.
1946–56: Regular conducting at Grant Park Concerts. (Eighty thousand people in attendance at one of his closing concerts of the season.)
1946: United States citizenship granted.
1948: Concert Tour, Israel, December 1948–January 1949.
1957: Permanent Conductor, Sydney, Australia, Symphony Orchestra. Occupied this position until his death in 1961.
1959: Guest Conductor, Soviet Union: Moscow, Leningrad, Kiev.
1960: Guest Conductor on Tour in Japan.
1961: Died, Sydney, Australia, June 23, 1961.
1965: The first *Nicolai Malko (Memorial) International Competition for Young Conductors* was held in Copenhagen, Denmark. The Copenhagen State Radio Orchestra was used for all sessions of the competition and it was under the patronage of the King.
1968 and 1971: The second and third Memorial Competitions took place, again honoring the memory of Nicolai Malko. Fourth competition, 1974.

A SAMPLING OF PRESS NOTICES FROM AROUND THE WORLD

Boston Post: The clarity of his (Malko's) readings was extraordinary, even in the mazes of Reger's polyphony: while euphony could scarcely go farther.

Chicago Daily News, July 18, 1941: One of history's great conductors. One of the greatest living conductors. *(Eugene Stimson)*

London Daily Telegraph, January 20, 1940: The orchestra has rarely played better.

Birmingham (England) *Evening Dispatch,* February 2, 1937: The finest performance of Tchaikovsky's Fourth Symphony I have ever heard.

Liverpool (England) *Echo:* Beethoven's Leonora Overture No. 3 which for sheer brilliance one would find it hard to equal.

Die Stunde (Vienna): A supreme master and interpreter.

Berliner Tageblatt (Berlin), February 27, 1932: A conductor of the highest rank. Never has the orchestra played with such precision before as it did under his baton.

Müncher Zeitung (Munich), February 21, 1930: Malko combines all the gifts that make a great conductor. Never have I heard Borodin's Second Symphony and Tchaikovsky's Fourth performed so masterly as at this concert.

Prager Presse (Prague), March 20, 1930: (Speaking of Moussorgsky's *Boris Godounov.*) The singers, carried away by Malko's inspiring baton, surpassed themselves.

Gazeta Warszawska (Warsaw), January 23, 1933: Malko is a great master of the baton . . . a truly great conductor.

El Telegrafo (Buenos Aires), July 7, 1929: The concert was in every way perfect . . . an endless ovation.

El Holger (Buenos Aires), August 16, 1929: Malko is one of the greatest personalities ever to conduct here.

Tokyo Shumbun, December 18, 1959: His arm movements are very spare but very exacting and clear, and he made the orchestra fantastic as never before.

The Mainichi (Japan), Sunday, December 27, 1959: . . . a triumphant success it was for the celebrated guest-conductor, and for the Japanese musicians too, as he succeeded in stretching, yet without ever straining, the frame of their capabilities far beyond the limits of what they had supposedly been able to do. . . . It was little short of a miracle. *(Kalus Pringsheim)*

Palestine Post (Israel), December 19, 1948 (Re: Shostakovitch First Symphony.) . . . it was a stirring performance to listen to so authentic an interpretation.

Sydney Morning Herald (Sydney, Australia), April 15, 1957: . . . one of the vintage concerts of recent seasons. Fine tone, fine sentiment, fine scruple in matters of balance, lucid textures—what more could you ask? *(L. B.)*

The Herald (Melbourne, Australia), September 5, 1957: . . . the performance of the Brahms Fourth Symphony was free from excesses and full of a deep and mature musicianship. I have never heard the second movement played more beautifully with layer after layer of poetry. *(John Sinclair)*

Daily Telegraph (Sydney, Australia), April 10, 1957: Malko wins audience . . . remarkable pianissimo achieved in the Beethoven and only possible to the most sensitive and experienced artist. *(Eunice Gardner)*

Irfun Olej Merkas Europa (Herbinblatt), January 7, 1949: In der Symphonie Aus der neuen Welt von Dvorak schuf der Dirigent Malko besonders in letzten Satze neue Klangwelt aus der grossartigen Susammenhaltung aller Klangenergie, doch ohne Nachteil für die Klarheit der

Stimmenführung. Seit Molinaris Eroica habe ich ahnliches hier nicht gehört. *(P. R.)*

Record News (London), September, 1957: Symphonie Nr. 5 in E Minor, Dvorak. Philharmonia Orchestra conducted by Nicolai Malko. HMV CLP 1125. I have not heard all the earlier recordings of this work but I find it hard to imagine a better one than this. . . . Malko moulds each phrase of this symphony with infinite care and precision, and these wonderful players all respond most devotedly; yet the music constantly moves forward in accordance with a well-conceived plan. Malko will often relax in order to allow a woodwind solo sufficient elbow room, but never to such extent that a violent wrench is needed in order to restore the basic tempo. I advise all who think that their adolescent pleasure in this work is gone beyond recall to try this recording. *(Anthony Roper)*

Kristelgt Dagblad (Copenhagen): (Speaking of a modern Danish composition.) Malko performed the work as perhaps he alone could do it. The importance of this man in music as an authentic interpreter can never be overrated.

Nationaltidende (Copenhagen): (Concerning *Oedipus Rex* by Stravinsky.) It was a performance that will remain unforgettable in its purity and unity. Nicolai Malko added with it new triumph to the many earlier ones.

Berlingske Tidende (Copenhagen): His clarity of thought throws light over the apparent darkness, so that out of a chaos comes organized Art.

ADDENDA TO THE MALKO BIOGRAPHY-CHRONOLOGY

There are still available recordings made under Malko's baton. In England these recordings come under the English His Master's Voice (HMV); likewise in Australia. The Danish recordings were made by the Scandinavian branch of HMV. Releases in the United States were handled by RCA Victor, Angel, and Blue Bird, and records have been issued in Japan and South America. Recently a fine Russian recording has been released.

As a teacher of conducting, Malko has largely "revolutionized" this field of instruction. His analytical knowledge of cause and effect from baton to player of the instrument has made an exact science of the technique of the stick. Not only had he thought through the technique itself (and tested it with orchestras all over the world), but he had also arranged it in teachable form, thus setting forth the order of technical development of the students. One who is well versed in the "Malko

School" can recognize instantly whether a conductor has a *knowledgeably* skilled technique in his hands or is relying largely upon natural talent to see him through. The conductor's hands should be no less skilled (trained) than those of the violinist or pianist. The technique is a bi-manual one, and the hands should be able to act with complete independence of each other. Malko knew how to achieve these results with his students, if they themselves would do the necessary practice technically.

Among leading conductors and teachers whom Malko has influenced may be named the following (all of whom had studied or coached with him for various periods of time): Eugene Mravinski (he brought the Leningrad Symphony to the United States on its tour here); Nicolai Rabinovich, Ilia Mussin, and Isai Sherman, professors of conducting at the Leningrad Conservatory; Leo Ginsburg, Professor of Conducting at the Moscow Conservatory; Boris Khaikin, Conductor at the Bolshoi Theater in Moscow and the teacher of Kondrashin, who toured the United States as conductor with the Moscow Symphony; Marjan Kozina (now deceased), former leading conductor of Yugoslavia and for a time conductor of the Philharmonic Orchestra in Lyubliana; A. Melik-Pashaev (now deceased), one of the great conductors of Russia at the Bolshoi Theater; Frank Peleg (deceased), Israel, Conductor in Haifa; Jens Schroeder, Conductor of the Aalborg Symphony, Denmark (he often conducts in the United States) Arne Hammelboe, Conductor of the Ballet at the Royal Theater in Copenhagen and Professor of Conducting at the Royal Danish Conservatory; Rudolf Michel, for many years chief conductor of Radio Saar, Germany; Juan Jose Castro (now deceased), outstanding Argentinian composer and conductor (he coached with Malko in 1929 when Malko toured South America). Among the Americans who worked with Malko at one time or another, here or in Salzburg, are: Samuel Barber, Thomas Schippers, Thor Johnson, Lawrence Sardoni, Irwin Kostal (Walt Disney Studios), John Barnett, Rex Maupin, George Oliver, Galichio, William Strickland, Harold Geerdes, Virginia Short, Lela Hanmer, Emerson Kailey, W. C. Byrd, and Elizabeth A. H. Green.

Malko's last pupil was (in Sydney, Australia) Helen Quach, the gifted young Chinese woman from Saigon who won first place in the Mitropoulos Competition in New York in 1967 and who has since toured Japan and the Philippines and is presently conducting the Ku-Ring-Gai Philharmonic Orchestra in Sydney. Miss Quach has conducted several times at the National Music Camp at Interlochen, Michigan—the "International Symphony."

APPENDIX F: Bibliography

Austin, William W., *Music in the Twentieth Century, From Debussy through Stravinsky.* New York: W. W. Norton & Co., Inc., 1966. Contains a magnificent bibliography of more than 100 pages on the composers discussed.

Behrman, D., "What Indeterminate Notation Determines," *Perspectives of New Music,* Spring-Summer, 1965, S 58–73.

Berry, Wallace, *Form in Music.* Englewood Cliffs, New Jersey: Prentice-Hall, Inc., 1966.

Blackman, Charles, *Behind the Baton.* New York: Charos Enterprises, Inc. (Carl Fischer, sole selling agent), 1964.

Boult, Sir Adrian C., *A Handbook on the Technique of Conducting.* Oxford, England: Hall the Printer, Ltd., 1936.

Braithwaite, Warwick, *The Conductor's Art.* London: Williams & Norgate, Ltd., 1952.

Brindle, Reginald Smith, *Serial Composition.* London: Oxford University Press, 1966.

Cage, John, *Notations.* New York: Something Else Press, 1969.

Carse, Adam von Ahn, *The Orchestra in the Eighteenth Century.* Cambridge, England: W. Heffer & Sons, Ltd., 1940.

———, *The Orchestra from Beethoven to Berlioz.* Cambridge, England: W. Heffer & Sons, Ltd., 1948.

Choate, Robert A., Barbara Kaplan, and James Standifer, *Sound, Beat and Feeling* from the *New Dimensions in Music Series.* New York: American Book Company, 1972, pp. 198–199.

———, *Sound, Shape and Symbol* from the *New Dimensions in Music Series.* New York: American Book Company, 1973, pp. 158–159.

Christiani, Adolf F., *Principles of Expression in Pianoforte Playing.* New York: Harper Brothers, 1886 (Broude).

Cooper, G. W., and L. B. Meyer, *The Rhythmic Structure of Music.* Chicago: The University of Chicago Press, 1960.

Cope, David, *New Directions in Music.* Dubuque, Iowa: William C. Brown Co., 1971.

Crocker, Richard L., *A History of Musical Style.* New York: McGraw-Hill Book Co., Inc., 1966

Eimert, Herbert, Fritz Enkel, and Karlheinz Stockhausen, *Problems of Electronic Notation,* trans. D. A. Sinclair. Ottawa: National Research Council of Canada, Technical Translation, TT 612, 1956.

Eimert, Herbert, and Karlheinz Stockhausen, *Die Reihe.* A periodical devoted to developments in contemporary music. Bryn Mawr, Pa.: Theodore Presser Co., in association with Universal Edition, London, Wien, Zurich.

Erickson, R., *"Time Relations," Journal of Music Theory,* Winter, 1963, pp. 174–192.

Fishback, Horace, III, *A Handbook of Musical Style.* Teaneck, N.J.: Fairleigh Dickinson University, 1966. Copyright by H. Fishback, III.

Fuchs, Peter Paul, *The Psychology of Conducting.* New York: MCA Music, A division of MCA, Inc., 1969.

Green, Elizabeth A. H., *The Modern Conductor.* Englewood Cliffs, N.J.: Prentice-Hall, Inc., 1961. Extensive manual technique and introduction to score study.

————, *Orchestral Bowings and Routines.* Ann Arbor, Mich.: Campus Publishers, 1949 and 1957. Copyright by E. A. H. Green.

Grosbayne, Benjamin, *Techniques of Modern Orchestral Conducting.* Cambridge: Harvard University Press, 1956.

Jacob, Gordon, *How to Read a Score.* London: Hawkes & Son, 1944. Boosey & Hawkes in the U.S.A.

Kahn, Emil, *Conducting.* New York: The Free Press, A division of Macmillan Company, 1965.

————, *Workbook for Conducting.* New York: The Free Press, A division of Macmillan Company, 1965.

Karkoschka, Erhard, *Das Schriftbild der neuen Musik.* Celle, Germany: Hermann Moeck Verlag, 1966.

Koenig, Ruth, *Notation in New Music, A critical guide to Interpretation and Realization.* Translated from the German by Ruth Koenig. New York: Frederick A. Praeger, Inc., 1972.

Machlis, Joseph, *Introduction to Contemporary Music.* New York: W. W. Norton & Co., Inc., 1961.

Malko, Nicolai, *The Conductor and His Baton.* Copenhagen: Wilhelm Hansen Verlag, 1950. Complete manual technique.

Marple, Hugo D., *The Beginning Conductor.* New York: McGraw-Hill Book Co., 1972.

McElheran, Brock, *Conducting Technique.* New York: Oxford University Press, 1966.

Melcher, Robert A., and Willard F. Warch, *Music for Score Reading.* Englewood Cliffs, N.J.: Prentice-Hall, Inc., 1971.

Meyer, Leonard B., *Emotion and Meaning in Music.* Chicago: Chicago University Press, 1956.

Morris, R. O., and Howard Ferguson, *Preparatory Exercises in Score Reading*. London: Oxford University Press, 1931.

Munch, Charles, *I am a Conductor*. New York: Oxford University Press, 1955.

Nallin, Walter E., *The Musical Idea*. New York: The Macmillan Co., 1968. Deals extensively with compositional forms and their development.

Perkins, J. M., *"Note Values," Perspectives in New Music*, Spring-Summer, 1963, pp. 47–57.

Read, Gardiner, *Thesaurus of Orchestral Devices*. New York: Pitman Publishing Corporation, 1953.

Standifer, James A. and Barbara Reeder, *Source Book of African and Afro-American Materials for the Music Educator*. Washington D.C.: Music Educators National Conference, 1974.

Seashore, Carl E., *Psychology of Music*. New York: McGraw-Hill Book Company, Inc., 1938.

Scherchen, Hermann, *Handbook of Conducting*, trans. M. P. Calvocoressi. London: Oxford University Press, 1933. A complete discussion of the instruments of the orchestra and their uses in orchestral works. Also some fine ear-training studies in the opening chapters.

Self, George, *New Sounds in the Class*. London: Universal Edition (London), Ltd., 1971.

Stanton, Royal, *The Dynamic Choral Conductor*. Delaware Water Gap, Pa.: Shawnee Press, Inc., 1971.

Stone, K., *"Problems and Methods of Notation," Perspectives of New Music*, Spring, 1963, pp. 9–31.

Tovey, Sir Donald Francis, *Essays in Musical Analysis* (six volumes). London: Oxford University Press, London and New York, 1935.

Wolf, J., *Handbuch der Notationskunde*, I, and II. Leipsig, 1913, 1919.

Note: The New York Public Library has set up an *Index of New Musical Notation*. (Lincoln Center, New York, N.Y.)

Indexes

Topical Index

Anecdotes
  Absurdities, 68
  Barbarolli, Sir John, with the Hallé Orchestra, 91
  Beecham, Sir Thomas, with ladies' choir, 97
  Coates' marking, 41–42
  Conductor threatens to leave, 98
  Irritable conductors, 92–93
  Klemperer and Bach, 70
  Malko, Nicolai:
    conducts Copenhagen Symphony, 30
    examines Cheribini score, 53
    feuds with Prokofieff, 103
    finds misprint in Holland, 52
    gives instructions for producing French horn forte, 125
  Mengelberg, Wilhelm, talking in rehearsal, 98
  Meyerhold:
    on quality, 24
    and *The Inspector General*, 105–6
  Netherlands symposium, 4
  Nikisch, Arthur, performing flute counterpoint, 26
  Rachmaninoff, Sergei, performing with Chicago Symphony, 51
  Richter, Hans:
    conducts in Grinzing, 92
    reprimands double-bass player, 97
  Schnabel, Artur, performing for music, 99
  Sousez, interpretations by, 105
  Strauss, Richard, erasing, 35
  Stravinsky, Igor:
    making changes in scores, 101–2
    style related to Haydn's, 23

Anecdotes (*cont.*)
  Suk, Vyacheslav:
    erases in *Russlan and Ludmilla* score, 34
    waits for D-flat in *Queen of Spades*, 53
Art:
  abstract, 107
  musical, 109, 110
  in space and time, 2
Artistry:
  amount of, 27
  in conductor's preparation, 94

Baton:
  as extension of arm, 127
  players' response to, 130
  range of expression, 22
  during talking, 129
  technique:
    appearance vs. sound, 128
    moment of pause, 129
    musical appearance, 127
    rebounds, 127, 129
    stress in, 130
Bowing:
  as accentuation, 69
  in Coriolanus, 70
  "naturale," 69
  in Oberon Overture, 58
  related to personality of orchestra, 68
  Russian vs. German, 68
  "spelled," 69, 70
  in Symphony in G Minor, 69–70
  unedited, 70
  uniformity of, 68

Charting the score, 83–88
Composer:
  and conductor, 21
  dynamics of, 48
  freedom of, 109
  "happenings," 109
  ideas of, 21, 49
  notation by, 21, 55
  reediting by, 102
  rights of, 13
  types of, 21
Conducting:
  mental side of, 9, 12
  moral aspects of, 9–10
  pedagogy:
    helping talented student, 130
    helping timid student, 129
  philosophy of, 106
  technique:
    ambiguity of, 127
    breathing, 128
    emotional tension in, 130
    an exact science, 125
    handling fermata, 128, 129
    independence of hands, 128
    leaning toward players, 128
    Malko's research on, 125
    moment of pause, 129
    monotony of, 128
    preparatory beat, 127
    rebounds, 127, 129
    starting and stopping, 126, 127
    using the arm, 95, 128
    using the left hand, 128
    wrist flexibility, 127
Conductor:
  attitude toward misprints, 51
  behavior in rehearsal, 92, 97, 98
  as builder, 94
  compared to public speaker, 27
  as controller, 7
  disposition of, 11
  dynamics of, 47
  as editor, 61
  function of, 126
  gestures of, 4, 13, 23, 93, 95, 108,
    113, 125, 140–58
    inventions in, 31, 109
  as guide, 7, 109
  his instruments, contact with, 9
  his job, 10

Conductor (*cont.*)
  mental preparation, 9, 12
  his musicians:
    contact with, 9, 11, 95
    dependency of, 96
    mishandling of, 92
    rapport with, 9, 10, 92, 93, 97
    rhythmic feeling of, 129
    spontaneous response of, 125
  phrasal consciousness of, 2
  planning the rehearsal, 7, 94
  rehearsing, 95
    gestures, 93
  responsibilities of, 10, 11
  retouching composer's notation, 51,
    56–60
  showing musicianship in interpreta-
    tion, 78
  his technical means, 95, 108
  technique, rehearsing of, 93, 109
Creative performance, 56
  in contemporary scores, 108, 109
Cues:
  contemporary, 109
  inaccurate, 21
  marking of, 41

Dynamics:
  adjustment of, 43, 47
    for composer's effect, 48, 49
    after tutti forte, 49
  of composer, 48
  crescendo after chord fermata, 26
  marking of, 41, 42, 114
  in phrasal analysis, 22
  types of, 47

Ear:
  development of, 3
  discovery of wrong notes, 53
  in Netherlands symposium, 4
  objective hearing, 2, 3, 92
  problems for, 2
  score markings for, 43
  in spontaneous hearing, 89
  subjective (imaginative) hearing, 2,
    3
  types of hearing, 3

Emotion in music, 12, 14, 77, 94
  varying response to, 82
Expression, means of, classified, 22
  Bruno Walter on, 27
Eye:
  of audience, 99
  contact with musicians, 89
  correlating rhythmic problems, 2
  score markings for, 43
  spontaneous proficiency of, 2

Fermata, 128, 129

Imagination:
  in interpretation, 2, 7, 77
  "interpretative," 77
  in performance, 108
  pictorial, 82
  in preliminary planning, 94
  training of, 78–82
Imitation, 10, 12
Instrumentation:
  adding or subtracting of, 43–46
  changes in, 43
  historical development, 43
  where missing, 32
  as printed, 32
Instruments:
  types of, 7
    dead, 8
    living, 8, 9
    voice, 8
Interpretation, 77–82
  building in rehearsal, 95, 97
  in contemporary works, 109
  through gesture, 31, 95, 140
  hints on, 78
  by simile, 96
  of specific works,¹ 102–6; 159–71
    The Impresario, 140–58
  Strauss: "Jupiter" Symphony, 71
Intonation, 4

Malko (*see also* Index of Names):
  chronology, 173
  press notices, 174–76
Marks, for conducting gestures, 70
Melos, defined, 77

Memorization:
  charting process, 83–88
  of *Les Portraits,* 103
  in pedagogy, 129
Memory:
  analytical, 77, 83
  reliance on melodic line, 83
  spontaneous, 77, 83, 89
  types of, 77
    contrasted, 82, 83
Mind, complexity of, 77
  in memorizing, 83
Music:
  as abstract art, 107
  content of, grasping, 12, 13
  emotionality of, 12, 13, 77, 82
  line of, 22
  as motion, 22, 95
  as situation, 109
  symbols, two meanings, 1
  from technique, 95
  as visual art, 14, 107, 110–13
Musical art, essence of, 99
Musical line, 22

Notation:
  as abstraction, 111, 122
  of composer, 21, 109
  confusion in, 51, 52, 109
  contemporary, 107, 109; Table 8–1,
    p 116
  density of, related to speed, 114
  in educational scores, 110, 118, 121
  individualized approach to, 110
  meaning of symbols in, 1, 107, 109
  misprints in, 51, 53, 54
  as miswritten by composer, 55
  size of related to dynamic, 114
  "spaced," 109, 122
  symbols, 122

Pedagogy, 125–30
Performance:
  coming alive, 10, 82
  creative, 24
  defects in, 23
  as goal, 99
  listening to, 12, 99
  mediocre, 26
  philosophy of, 99, 106

Performance *(cont.)*
   quality of, 26, 27, 78
     best, defined, 10
     related to style, 26
Phrase:
   dynamics of, 22
   expression of, 22
   horizontal extension of, 2
   interpreting of, 22
   leading of, 2, 22
Phrasing:
   analysis of, 14
     imperative, 35
   as bowing, 69
   charting of, 14, 15
   counting of, 35, 37
     introduced by up-beat, 38
   interlocking, 40, 140
   marking in score, 35
   numbering measures of, 35
   as syntax of score, 35
   three-measure form, 140
Pitch imagination, building of, 3

Rehearsals:
   goal of, 94
   planning of, 93, 94
   tempo of, 93
   timing of, 93
   types of, 91
Rehearsing:
   stopping the orchestra, 95
   talking vs. gesture, 96, 98
   two types of, 91
Repertoire, 140–72
Rhythm, building solidity of, 94, 128
Rhythmic feeling of players, 129

Score:
   analysis of, 14
   approaches to, 23
     mental, 12, 14
   charting of, 14–19, 83
     for memorizing, 83
     for phrasing, 14
   contemporary format, 113
   content of music, 13
   defacing of, 31
   divided, 33, 34

Score *(cont.)*
   as guidance chart, 7
   marking:
     changing the score, 43
     clarity of, 31
     in colors, 42
     in dangerous places, 31, 42
     of gestures, 30, 70
     purpose of, 32
     types of, 32
   memorizing, 83
   notation of *(see* Notation)
   problems of, 13
   proofreading, 50
   rationalization of, 14
   reading:
     horizontal, 2
     vertical, 2
     eye and ear, 2
   solo line, 33
   study:
     Brussels outline, 27
     expression, 22, 77
     instrumentation, 13
     mental aspect, 12, 14
     at the piano, 28
Scores, educational, 110
Sound:
   composer's delineation of, 13, 14
   idealized, 2
   non-musical, 108
   resultant of notated dynamics, 48
Style, defined, 23
   Malko's notes on, 172–73
   related to quality of performance, 26
Symbols *(see also* Notation):
   interpreting their meaning, 13

Talking, 96, 98
   baton position during, 129
Technical means related to artistic demands, 95
Technique, 140–72 *(See also* Baton):
   building of, 126–28
   controls in pedagogical order, 126–27
   defined, 126
   excess of, 27
   knowledgeable, 177
   left hand, 128

Tempo transitions, 25
Time-beating:
  ambiguous, 127
  for contemporary scores, 108, 113
  irregular, 108
  as "signal," 109, 113, 123
Tone colors, 108, 138, 139
  in strings:
    harmonics, 138
    ponticello, 139

Tradition:
  acceptance of, 12
  bad, 12, 24
Transposition, 133–37
  Table of, 136–37

Violin Concerto, Op. 36 (Schoenberg),
  32

Index of Names Mentioned in the Text

Barbarolli, Sir John, 91
Beecham, Sir Thomas, 51, 97
Beethoven, Ludwig Van, 23, 43
Blackman, Charles, 126
Boris Godounov, 53
Borowski, Felix, 53
Boult, Sir Adrian, 91
Bronnum restaurant, 101
Brussels Conservatory, 27
Cherubini, Luigi, 53
Coates, Albert, 41, 68
Copenhagen Competition, 96
Debussy, Claude, 57
Doboujinsky, 27
Engle, Fru, 35
Furtwangler, 94
Gingold, 69
Glazounov, Alexander, 51
Glebov, Igor, 105
Gogol, Nikolai, 105
Haydn, Franz Joseph, 23
Horowitz, Vladimir, 57
Jonas, G., 54
Kalinikoff, 31
Khaikin, B., 53
Kharkov, 68
Kiev, 31
Kleiber, Eric, 54
Klemperer, Otto, 69, 70
Kolar, Victor, 96
Lange, Hans, 69
Leningrad, 69
Liszt, Franz, 23, 57
Mahler, Gustav, 61, 68, 95
Malko, Nicolai, 2, 26fn, 30, 38, 52, 53,
    106, 173–76

Manchester, 9
Mariinsky Theater, 34, 41
Mengelberg, Wilhelm, 98
Meyerhold, 24, 105
Miaskovsky, Nicolai, 105
Moscow, 34
Mottl, Felix, 51
Mozart, Wolfgang Amadeus, 23
Napravnik, Eduard, 31
Netherlands Symposium, 4
Nikisch, Arthur, 26, 56, 59, 60, 91, 97
Orchestras:
    Berlin Philharmonic, 69
    Chicago Symphony, 49, 51, 69
    Cleveland Symphony, 70
    Concertgebouw Orchestra, 98
    Detroit Symphony, 96
    Hallé Orchestra (Manchester), 91
Penderecki, Krzysztof, 108
Prague, 70
Prokofieff, Serge, 103
Rachmaninoff, Sergei, 51
Reiner, Fritz, 49
Richter, Hans, 92, 97
Rimsky-Korsakoff, Nikolai, 68
Rose, 69
St. Petersburg, 31, 51
Schnabel, Artur, 99
Schoenberg, Arnold, 32, 107
Sibelius, Jean, 23
Stock, Frederick, 68
Strauss, Richard, 35, 49, 71
Stravinsky, Igor, 23, 101, 107
Suk, Vyacheslav 34, 51, 53
Szell, George, 69, 70

Toscanini, Arturo, 50, 52, 57, 68, 97, 98, 127

United States, 23

Verdi, Giuseppe, 52

Vienna, 97

Vinogradsky, A. N., 30, 31

Wagner, Richard, 77

Walter, Bruno, 27, 92

Webern, Anton, 107

Wood, Sir Henry, 51

Ziloti, 102

Zweig, 70

Index to Musical Examples, Charts, and Tables

Bach (*with Abert*):
  Prelude, Chorale, and Fugue, measures, 1–59, 150–55
Bartók:
  Concerto for Orchestra, first movement, Chart I, 15–19
Bedford:
  Whitefield Music, 119
Beethoven:
  Lenore Overture, No. 3, 44
  Symphony No. 1, first movement, 47
  Symphony No. 5, second movement, 54
  Symphony No. 7
    first movement, 47
      Mahler editing, 62, 64, 66
      original scoring, 63, 65, 67
    second movement, 55
    third movement, 43
Borodin:
  Symphony No. 2
    first movement, 20, 38
    finale, 42
Brahms:
  Symphony No. 4
    first movement, 36, 45
    second movement, 46

Dennis:
  Tetrahedron, 121
Dvořák:
  Slavonic Dance, Op. 72, No. 3, 140, 147–49
  Symphony No. 5
    first movement, 48
    third movement, 24, 25

Green:
  Expressive Phrases, 78-82

Hodkinson:
  Score set-up from *Contemporary Primer for Band,* 115

Instruments (transpositions), Table A-1, 136–37

Liszt:
  Les Preludes, 41
Logothetis:
  Cycloide, 111

Mahler:
  Symphony No. 5 in C-sharp minor, first movement, 141–46
Moron:
  Four Visions, 112
Mozart:
  Cosi Fan Tutte Overture, 40; Chart II, 83–86; Chart III, 87–88; Chart IV, 88–89
  The Impressario Overture, 21
  Symphony in G minor, K 550, first movement, 69
  Symphony in C major (Jupiter), K 551
    first movement, 49, 71–75
    fourth movement, 25

Rossini:
  William Tell Overture, 53

Schubert:
  Symphony No. 7, fourth movement, 50, 51
Score-line separation, 34
Score format, contemporary, 114
Score notation symbols, contemporary, Table I, 116–18

Self:
  Holloway, 120
Stravinsky:
  Firebird Suite, 26
Tchaikovsky:
  Francesca da Rimini, 33
  Romeo and Juliet Overture-Fantasy, 52
  Symphony No. 4, second movement, 26

Symphony No. 6, first movement, 60

Wagner:
  Tannhauser Overture, 44
  Tristan and Isolde, Prelude, 39

von Weber:
  Der Freischutz Overture, 45, 56
  Oberon Overture, 55, 57, 58, a and b, 59

REPERTOIRE OUTLINE NOTES

Beethoven: *Egmont* Overture, 161–62
  Symphony No. 1, fourth movement, 159–60
  Symphony No. 5, first movement, 160–61

Hayden: Symphony No. 104 (London), first movement, 162-64

Mendelssohn: Symphony No. 4 (Italian), 172

Schubert:
  Rosamunde Overture, 165–66
  Symphony No. 8 (Unfinished), 164–65
Strauss, J.: *Tales of the Vienna Woods,* 166–67

Tchaikovsky: *Romeo and Juliet* Overture-Fantasy, 167–70

von Weber: *Oberon* Overture, 170–71